2022
PASSION
PLAY

OBERAMMERGAU

Translated from the German by: Juan Lucas Cruz
                                 Saco Lesevic
Proofread by: Emily Pickerill
Graphic design: Otto Dzemla, München
Photographer Cover: Gabriela Neeb
Type setting and Printed by: Kriechbaumer Druck
                                 GmbH & Co. KG, München

Published by: Gemeinde Oberammergau
Copyright: Gemeinde Oberammergau

978-3-9824552-1-1

2022
PASSION
PLAY
OBERAMMERGAU

Using the Oberammergau Play texts by Othmar Weis, O.S.B. (1769-1843) and the Reverend Joesph Alois Daisenberger (1799-1883) For the 2022 play extensively edited and expanded by Christian Stückl.

The text of the Passion Play was written by Christian Stückl, using older play texts.
The lyrics were edited by Otto Huber.

The Oberammergau Passion music,
1811-20 composed by Rochus Dedler (1779-1822),
1950 edited by Prof. Eugen Papst (1886-1956).
Since 2000 newly revised and expanded
by Markus Zwink.

FOREWORD

The Oberammergau Passion Play is a very special play. It all started with a vow. In 1633, the plague was raging in Europe, including in the town of Oberammergau. People sought refuge in prayer and vowed: If the dying stops, every ten years we will stage the "play of the passion, death, and resurrection of our Lord Jesus Christ. "And in fact, no one died of the plague from that day on. Since then, the people of Oberammergau have been performing the Passion of Jesus Christ every ten years. For 200 years, the play was staged on the cemetery near the church. However, in the 19th century, when more and more people started coming from all over the world to see the play, it was moved to the place where the Passion Theatre (built in 1900) stands today. While there are manifold reasons why so many people want to see the play, one reason certainly has to do with the special character of this play. It revolves around the mystery of the Passion of Jesus in a dramatic as well as meditative way. Between scenes, moments from the Old Testament come alive as theatrical depictions of related situations from earlier times. They also serve as meditative points of reflection throughout the play. As in 2000 and 2010, these living pictures for 2022 were designed and organized by Stefan Hageneier who also designed the costumes and had the stage rebuilt to achieve stylistic unity.

Moreover, thanks to its poignant musical score composed by Rochus Dedler (1779-1822), the play is performed more like an oratory. For newly staged parts, Markus Zwink has added some longer intervals. He is entrusted with the musical direction of the choir, orchestra and soloists in 2022 (as he was in 1990, 2000 and 2010).
The original text of the play was written by Pastor

Joseph Daisenberger (1799–1883). However larger passages have already been changed for the last three performances. The current production also has many rewritten parts of the original text, which Christian Stückl (director since 1990) often reformulates even during rehearsals. In addition to participating residents of Oberammergau, he also sought advice from representatives of Jewish organizations who have shown great interest in the fact that the play correctly depicts unique religious and cultural aspects of the Jewish religion, to avoid the anti-Semitic overtones coming to the fore, as has occurred far too often in history. The people of Oberammergau fully support this goal.

THE 2022 PLAY

Due to the pandemic, the performance had to be postponed from 2020 to 2022. The new production aims to update the dramatic art of the play in a contemporary way (similar to the performances of 1990, 2000 and 2010). There are multiple reasons for this. The audience today is different than the spectators twenty-two or even twelve years ago. Many people are no longer familiar with the theological details that were considered common knowledge in earlier times. The questions we have to ask have changed. Since the Passion Play seeks to convey the message of the passion, death and resurrection of Jesus Christ to people as a reassuring and empowering event, it must take up the fears and hopes of people today. Thus, in the depiction of Christ's suffering and death, the questions regarding the meaning and future of human existence come into view in dramatic ways. The new production aims to clarify important elements of Jesus' message for today's spectators. As in the 2010 production, Jesus does not immediately begin to drive the merchants and money changers out of the temple after his entry into the city and the temple, but first introduces himself as the Messiah who aims to renew the religious faith of his people and make the message of God its centerpiece. Quotations from Jesus' speeches (especially from the Sermon on the Mount) as well as from other biblical passages clarify his fundamental position. This also results in a social claim that includes a commitment to a just society. However, Jesus does not want to redeem this politically (superficially), but religiously, which means: He wants to change people's hearts. Only after Jesus' core message has become clear in the play does he chase the merchants out of the temple and thus cleanses the sanctuary of commerce and worldly business.

In particular, the historical situation takes center stage in the play. The Jewish people were politically and often socially repressed as well by the Roman occupying power. From the very beginning, Roman soldiers are therefore visible during the play, and a tense atmosphere is palpable in the room. Pilate, the Roman governor, also appears before the trial and puts pressure on the high priest Caiaphas; he tries to ensure a peaceful outward appearance in the context of religious activities. In the trial itself, Pilate cynically mocks Jesus' powerlessness as much as the Jewish religion as a whole.

Within the High Council, the supreme religious authority at the time, Jesus' condemnation is more fiercely debated than in previous productions.

The followers of Jesus are more present and argue confidently against the enemies.

The tragedy surrounding the figure of Judas is also made clearer. He is the betrayed traitor. Caiaphas deceives him about the consequences of handing over Jesus. Judas only wants to force a meeting of Jesus with the High Council so that Jesus' messages of the kingdom of God can be pushed forward more politically; by no means does he seek his death. He regrets his actions and throws the money he was given into the temple. He had not expected this as a reward, it was only given to him as a bonus after the betrayal.

Judas does not believe in forgiveness—he cannot forgive himself, does not expect forgiveness from anyone, not even from Jesus—and he takes refuge in death as a desperate man.

The betrayal of Peter, who denies Jesus in order not to get himself into trouble, takes place in parallel to the betrayal of Judas. When Peter realizes his failure, he regrets it. But he reacts differently to Judas. While Judas hangs himself, Peter weeps bitterly and finds new trust in Jesus through his grief. He knows: God will forgive me! He leaves the stage with his head held high.

Similar to 2010, the final scene is staged in a manner reflecting the liturgy. Jesus is carried to his grave, but it is not visible. This eliminates the depiction of the guards at the tomb. An angel tells the women: "Why do you seek the living among the dead? He is not here, he has risen." The Risen Lord appears only briefly. Mary of Magdala then announces: „I know that my Savior lives!" The tribute to the celebration of light during the Easter Vigil Mass, the music and reserved visual staging emphasize the character of the numinous and incomprehensible holiness. Thus, the final scene of the play emphasizes the theological principle: the resurrection is a „mystery of faith."

ACKNOWLEDGMENT

The 2022 production has once again heavily revised the Passion text written by Joseph Daisenberger with the intention of presenting the following matter more clearly: Jesus, the Jew, wanted to renew the religion of the fathers. He acted prophetically. With religious zeal, he calls upon people to promote social justice and to take religion seriously in its innermost core, which means: cultivating the relationship to the Eternal Father — God— and to prove this through acts of social justice. Simply put, Jesus emphasizes that: „praying" and „loving" are crucial in the Jewish / Christian religion, while everything plays a more supportive role.

The people of Oberammergau have tackled the Passion Play of 2022 with the same enormous commitment as they have done in the decades before. They know their duty. They keep the vow of their ancestors in a way that fulfils the aim of the promise at that time, namely, to strengthen confidence and faith for the future. So, the play is not a „popular theater of bygone times." It is a „theater of the people for the people" that seeks to convey hope.

LUDWIG MÖDL

Prof. Dr. Ludwig Mödl, currently pastor at the „Heilig-Geist-Kirche" in Munich, (serves once more, as in 2000 and 2010, as) theological advisor of the Oberammergau Passion Play 2022 (on behalf of Archbishop Reinhard Cardinal Marx in consultation with the Protestant Regional Bishop Heinrich Bedford — Strohm).

THE OBERAMMERGAU PLAY OF THE PASSION OF JESUS OF NAZARETH

PRELUDE

„The first decades of the 17th century passed in happy peace for Oberammergau. But then came the extremely distressing time of the Thirty Years' War, which was fought from 1618 to 1648, and whose memory still lives on among the people, now known as the Swedish Intervention. As early as 1631, infectious diseases struck both Swabia and Bavaria. The local village was protected from contagion by diligent vigilance until the church fair in 1632, when a local man named Kaspar Schisler brought the plague into the village. In their sorrow over the suffering this terrible disease had brought to the community, the leaders of the community came together and made a vow to hold the Passion Tragedy every ten years, and from that time on not a single person died."

THE EXPULSION
FROM PARADISE

CHOIR

> Lord, you are far away! We are astray,
> without a home, born to die,
> neighbors but strangers, divided by walls,
> orphaned, in tears and in mourning!

SOLOISTS AND CHOIR

> Lord, let the humble walk upright!
> Be the fountain for the thirsty
> and let us see in the sleep of death
> above us your face so bright!

BASS — SOLO

> Mankind despairs,
> despondent in toil and sorrow
> and longs for the time,
> ere from paradise
> the angel cast them out and banished them.
>
> Mankind is banned from Eden's meadows,
> benighted by delusions and in the horror of death.
> Mankind's access to the tree of life is, alas, obstructed;
> the cherub standing there, threatening with the
> flaming sword.
> But from afar, from the top of the mount of Calvary
> a morning glow shines through the night,
> and from the branches of the cross
> travel winds of peace across the world.

CHOIR

> Now stand side by side with the Savior,
> until he has battled his way through the thorny path
> and in his torrid conflict
> has finished suffering for us all!

ENTRY INTO JERUSALEM

PEOPLE AND CHILDREN

    Hail, hail to you, O Son of David!
    The Fathers' throne is yours to take!
    You, who comes in the name of the Most High,
    welcomed by all of Israel —
    you we praise, you we praise!
    Hosanna! He who dwells in heaven,
    He sends all grace upon you!
    Hosanna! May He who sits on the heaven's throne,
    preserve you for us eternally!
    Hail, hail to you, O Son of David!
    The Fathers' throne is yours to take!
    You, who comes in the name of the Most High,
    welcomed by all of Israel —
    you we praise, you we praise!
    Hosanna to our Son of the King!
    Let our words travel with the winds afar!
    Hosanna! On the throne of David
    may he reign in majesty!
    Hail to you! Hail to you, O Son of David!
    The Fathers' throne is yours to take!
    You, who comes in the name of the Most High,
    welcomed by all of Israel —
    you we praise, you we praise.

JUDAS

    Hosanna!

PEOPLE

    Hosanna!

PETER

    Blessed be the Anointed One!

PEOPLE

    Blessed be the Anointed One! Hosanna!

JESUS

    Come! Come to me, all who labor and are heavy
    burdened! Come, all who are weakened by the burden
    of misfortune and sorrow! We are living in a time
    of fear in Israel. War cries echo through the land,
    poverty and disease ravage you, and you hunger and

thirst for justice. The LORD hears your cries. He sees your misery, your fear and your distress. — I have come to comfort you, to heal your broken hearts.

NATHANAEL

What do you want? Why did you come?

JESUS

I have come to proclaim freedom for the captives and liberation for those who are bound.

EZEKIEL

I think it is better you leave.

ARCHELAUS

Beware, for he is a false prophet. He flatters you!

EZEKIEL

His words will not satisfy your hunger!

JESUS

They are hungry, but you give them nothing to eat! They are thirsty, but you give them nothing to drink! The strangers you do not receive, and the naked you do not clothe! When someone is naked and suffers hunger every day, and you say: Go in peace! — But do not give him what his body needs — what good will that do him? — You rich, weep and wail over the misery that will come upon you! You have already received your reward. You who are satisfied now — you will suffer hunger. You who are laughing now – you will mourn and cry. Your wealth will rot and your clothes will be eaten by moths. *(To the poor)* Arise, you innocent who are persecuted. God will bestow the land upon you! Arise, you who live in poverty, to you belongs the kingdom of God. Arise, you who weep now; for shall laugh.

ARCHELAUS

Silence! Who gave you permission to speak in the temple?

PEOPLE

We want to hear him!

JESUS

I tell you: Blessed are the merciful, for they shall receive mercy. Blessed are those pure in heart, for they shall see God. Blessed are the peacemakers, for they shall be called children of God.

DATHAN

The High Priest!

CAIAPHAS

Beautiful words, Jesus of Nazareth! You speak as if you were carrying the Spirit of the Lord. I ask you: What is this dream you are dreaming?

JESUS

It is not a dream! If God were your king, the poor would enjoy happiness in abundance.

CAIAPHAS

God is my king.

PETER

Then do not close your eyes to their misery!

JOHN

Whoever shows mercy to their fellow people will be shown mercy in heaven.

JESUS

Caiaphas, rethink your beliefs! Listen to your voice. Take care of your sheep. Find the lost. Bring back those who have strayed. Care for the wounded. Strengthen the weak. Be merciful as God our Father is merciful.

NATHANAEL

Enough! We come before God's face in holiness and righteousness!

EZEKIEL

We fast. We give to those in need!

JUDAS

No! You are blind and deaf! God has chosen those who are poor in the eyes of the world, but you condemn them.

JESUS

You do not strengthen the weak, you do not heal the sick, you do not care for the wounded, you do not bring back the lost, and you do not look for those who have strayed.

JAMES A.

What was robbed from the poor lies in your homes.

ARCHELAUS

How dare you? If anyone thinks he serves God but does not keep his tongue in check, their faith is void!

NATHANAEL

A false prophet he is, leading you astray.

PETER

No! You have wronged the poor.

JESUS

Look at them, they are tired and exhausted like sheep without a shepherd.

JUDAS

Is it not the rich who are violent against you and are taking you to court?

SOME

He speaks the truth...We suffer hunger...Our children are starving

EZEKIEL

Silence! Wealth and honor come from God; He rules over everything. In His hand lies strength and power, in His hand lies the power to make everyone great and strong.

PETER

Indeed, while one man lives in freshness and health, with all wealth and without a care, the other one dies with a bitter soul and has never tasted happiness. Is that your belief?

ANNAS

Do not listen to them! Do not listen to those who tell you what you want to hear. Jesus of Nazareth is a friend of tax collectors and harlots! A friend of sinners!

JESUS

Why do you condemn people? Who are you to judge your neighbor?

ANNAS

We come before God in holiness and righteousness, but you are a friend of tax collectors and harlots and dare to forgive their sins!

EZEKIEL

Who can forgive sins except for the one true God?

ANNAS

The Lord said: „ I will be gracious to whom I will be gracious, and will show mercy on whom I will show mercy. "

PETER

Yes, but then why do you judge your brother? Or you, why do you condemn your brother? We will all be brought before the judgment of God.

CAIAPHAS

Speak! Why do you loiter around the houses of the impure, the harlots, and dine with tax collectors?

JESUS

I tell you, no man is impure!

ANNAS

I see: Tax collectors and harlots will enter the kingdom of God before we do.

EZEKIEL

How can you eat with those who collect the hated taxes and drive our people into poverty and despair?

ARCHELAUS

Speak! Is it right to pay taxes to the emperor?

NATHANAEL

Answer! Tell us here before the people, that they may hear: Shall our subjugation continue, shall we go on with paying gold to Rome?

ARCHELAUS

Speak! Answer! Should we pay or not?

PETER

Careful now!

SOME OF THE PEOPLE

Yes ... yes ... answer... speak ... shall we continue to pay.

JESUS

Why put me to the test? Bring me a coin and let me look at it! – Whose likeness and inscription is it?

NATHANAEL

That of the emperor.

JESUS

Then give to the emperor the things that are the emperor's, and to God the things that are God's! You hypocrites, you honor God only with your lips, yet your heart is far from Him.

JEHOSHAPHAT

Rabbi, what good can I do to achieve eternal life?

JAMES A.

You are a teacher of Israel and you do not know that?

PETER

Follow the commandments!

JEHOSHAPHAT

You shall not murder; you shall not commit adultery; you shall not steal; you shall not bear false witness; honor your father and mother, and love your neighbor as yourself. I have followed them all; what am I missing?

JESUS

Sell everything you have and give it to the poor...

JEHOSHAPHAT

(laughs) "Sell everything you have and give it to the poor "... Well, then how can anybody be saved?

NICODEMUS

Woe to you — you do not know hunger and laugh at those who are hungry. You will receive your reward.

JESUS

Before you enter the kingdom of God, a camel will go through the eye of a needle. Rethink your beliefs! Do not gather wealth on earth that will be eaten away by moths and rust. Gather treasures in heaven! Because where your treasure is, there your heart will be also. Direct all your cares, all your actions and aspirations to the kingdom of God and his righteousness!

CAIAPHAS

Jesus, Rabbi, I see that you are solely concerned with the truth. You do not tell people what they want to hear — no matter how high their standing is. You freely tell us that we should live according to God's will. But you yourself have defiled the Sabbath! Have you not? Did you not heal on a Sabbath? You and your followers are doing what God has forbidden!

JESUS

Why are you so outraged that I healed a person on a Sabbath? Would anyone who owns a single sheep not grab it and pull it out if it falls into a pit on a Sabbath? How much more is a human life worth compared to that of a sheep? Caiaphas, the Sabbath was created for the people, not the people for the Sabbath. That is why it is permitted to do good on the Sabbath.

NATHANAEL

What is this? A new doctrine?

CAIAPHAS

Are you the master of the Sabbath? God has given us his word, but you are overruling the tradition of our ancestors.

ANNAS

Why do your disciples transgress the traditions of our ancestors? They do not wash their hands before they eat.

JESUS

You blind guides who sift out gnats but swallow camels!

NATHANAEL

Did you not read: They shall wash their hands and their feet, so that they may not die. This is an eternal order for Moses, his lineage and their descendants.

JEHOSHAPHAT

Why are you so ignorant?

JESUS

Listen and understand! It is not what goes into our mouths that makes us impure! Do you not realize that everything that goes into your mouth goes through your belly and falls into the pit? But whatever comes out of your mouth, evil words, false testimony and blasphemy, those make us impure. We use our tongue to praise the Lord, and curse the people. This is what makes us impure! Not unwashed hands! Keep your traditions — wash yourselves, cleanse yourselves! But get evil out of my sight! Stop doing wrong! Learn to do good, put those who oppress others in their place! Give orphans and widows back their rights!

JOSEPH OF ARIMATHEA

Whoever condemns his neighbor is a sinner. Blessed are those who have mercy on the poor.

NATHANAEL

Apostates and sinners break down. Those who forsake the Lord are finished.

ANNAS

Do not believe this dreamer! — Say, how can he understand the Scriptures when he has not studied them? We priests alone have been given the task of proclaiming God's will to you.

NATHANAEL

But he wants to undermine the law that God gave us through Moses.

CAIAPHAS

No, he twists the words to his purpose. — Now, let us see how serious you are about the Law of Moses. See: This woman was caught in the act of adultery. In his Law, Moses commands us to stone such a woman. He spoke: „They shall bring her out to the front of the house, and the people of the city shall stone her to death, because she has committed an abomination in Israel and has played the harlot. "What do you say to this?

(Jesus is silent)

ANNAS

She is an irrepressible woman, seductive, and has no shame.

EZEKIEL

Her reckless harlotry has made the land impure.

CAIAPHAS

Why does your courage abandon you here?

NATHANAEL

He keeps his own word: Judge not, lest you be judged.

JEHOSHAPHAT

Cold sweat on his forehead.

CAIAPHAS

He is silent. So I ask you: Should I show her mercy?

PTOLEMY

Stone her!

SOME

Stone her!

OTHERS

Stone her!

AGAIN OTHERS

Stone her!

JESUS

Yes, stone her... but let him who is without sin cast the first stone.

(Caiaphas leaves the square)

NATHANAEL

Caiaphas?

JUDAS

Hosanna!

PEOPLE

Hosanna!

JUDAS

Blessed be the Anointed One!

SOME

Blessed be the Anointed One! Hosanna!

JESUS

Where are your accusers now?

ADULTEROUS WOMAN

They all left. And no one has judged me.

JESUS

Then I do not judge you either. Go and sin no more!

JUDAS

Hosanna!

PEOPLE

Hosanna!

THE HUMILIATION OF THE ISRAELITES

TENOR — SOLO

Soon the hour is approaching,
when Jesus' mission is fulfilled —
as once from the prophets' mouths
the will of God was revealed.
„With your sacrifices, "said the Lord,
„I am no longer pleased —
people's hearts is my desire!
In obedience to me they shall live!
They shall give themselves fully to me! "

And Jesus gives himself to the point of death!
Neither fear nor distress
can separate him from God's will!
Who hears his word,
will see the right way!
Just as Moses once —
guided by God's Word —
did lead his people out of exile,
will Jesus now prepare the way for us,
that will be a blessing,
to everyone who walks it.

CHOIR

O Lord, hear the plea of your people in a foreign land!
O Lord, let us see salvation! Save us with a strong
hand!
Lord, see our plight!
See our misery in Egypt's slavery!
Help us escape from the Pharaoh's prison,
who — as an act of mockery against you —
has pressed your people into servitude
and does not let them go in peace!

God of our fathers,
show us anew

your eternal allegiance!
Be our savior!
Hear our sorrow!
Break our chains!
With your strong hand
lead us to the Promised Land!
Stand with us in this night!
O Lord, free us from our slave's shackles!

JESUS IN BETHANY

Scene 1

LAZARUS
Mary! Martha! Simon, he is coming!

SIMON OF BETHANY
Rabbi! It is a pleasure that you have accepted my invitation and graced my house with your presence!

PETER
Simon, the day is finally approaching when he will restore the kingdom of Israel and free it from the Romans.

JUDAS
Encouraged by his success in entering the Holy City, the people will proclaim him King of Israel and raise him to David's throne.

BARTHOLOMEW
His reign will be great and there will be no end to peace.

THOMAS
Over David's kingdom he will reign. Strengthened in righteousness and justice.

JUDAS
And every soldier's boot that comes pounding and every coat that is stained with blood will be burned and consumed by fire. The yoke of oppression, the bar on our shoulders and the rod of our oppressors you will break as in the day of Midian.

JESUS

Judas, your thoughts are not my thoughts, and your ways are not my ways.

JUDAS

You will judge the godless.

JESUS

Judas, I have not come to judge the world. I have come so that the world may be saved.

JUDAS

Rabbi, the day of our longing has finally come. Rise up! Be our King, lead the way and do not allow the righteous to be executed!

THOMAS

If you lead us, the people will rise up and we will drive the wretched Romans out of our land.

THADDAEUS

Judas is right! The people are on our side.

SIMON OF BETHANY

Do you yearn for war? Is war such a precious thing that you glorify it? Is it so gracious that you long for it?

LAZARUS

Why call for war? Why wake up the ravenous beast with your clamor? Clear your mind, Judas, stop before you run into darkness!

MAGDALENE

Is your subjugation so hard, is your suffering so burdensome? Judas look around you: God's sun is shining over the land, and your vines are blossoming in peace.

SIMON OF BETHANY

War is an evil beast, and with its hooves it tramples the land.

JUDAS

Simon, no one yearns for war, but should we endure this forever? When we are robbed, we tolerate it; when we are beaten, we remain silent; and even for those who are murdered, we dare not sigh aloud!

ANDREAS

Are the people of Israel born as slaves or born with shackles, that they may be the owned by the Romans? Jesus, the city is full of refugees who have left their villages for fear of the Romans.

JUDAS

Do not close your eyes to their distress!

MATTHEW

Judas is right, the Romans are consuming our land and our harvest!

JUDAS

Speak, answer, here before us tell us, that we may hear it: shall we be silent and live in servitude, shall we go on with paying taxes to those cursed Romans?

SIMON THE ZEALOT

Are we to just helplessly watch as the Romans spit on us?

THOMAS

Why are we still hesitating? Why do we not resist?

JESUS

Trust in God!

PETER

Do not laugh! He is right! Trust in the Lord who led us out of Egypt, who guided us through the desert and brought us to a fruitful land!

JUDAS

Yes, Peter but God used his strong hand and chased the Pharaoh's soldiers into the depths of the sea.

THOMAS

Yes! He gave the Pharaoh to the sea and threw him into the darkness of death.

JUDAS

God's wrath shall be revealed against all ungodly beings and all of humanity's injustice.

JESUS

Clear your minds! Turn your heart to the Lord and serve Him alone!

JUDAS

I serve God, but I do not serve subjugation. Is it not written: An eye for an eye and a tooth for a tooth?

JESUS

> Yes, it is written. I tell you: Stand up to those who do evil to you! But do it like this: If someone slaps you on the right cheek, turn the other one to him as well!

ANDREAS

> Who can listen to this?

JOHN

> It is written: „In rest you will be saved; staying calm and trusting will be your strength. "

JESUS

> When I am weak, then I am strong.

JAMES Z.

> And if he rips off my tunic, then I shall give him my coat as well?

JESUS

> Yes! And if a Roman forces you to go one mile with him, go two with him! Love your neighbor as you love yourself!

JUDAS

> I will love my neighbor. But with equal fervor, I will hate the Romans.

JESUS

> If you love the one who loves you, have you achieved a special feat? Do heathens not do the same? Clear your minds! Be children of your Father in heaven! He makes his sun rise on the good and the evil, and sends rain down on the righteous and the unrighteous. Love your enemies, bless those who curse you, do good to those who hate you, and pray for those who insult and persecute you!

THOMAS

> The Romans beat us and we are supposed to pray for them and love them? Never!

SEVERAL APOSTLES

> Never!

Scene 2

JEHOSHAPHAT

Do not listen to him! He will not free Israel from the Romans. He is a weakling and fears the sword.

JUDAS

I will not let my anger be taken away, my hand remains outstretched.

JESUS

Let go of your anger! Do not allow yourselves to get enraged, it only leads to evil. People's anger does not lead to what is right in the sight of God. There is famine in the land. The land is filled with war and the cries of soldiers. One nation rises against another and one kingdom against another. Many will fall, they will betray each other and hate each other. One sibling will give up his brother to death, and the father his child, and the children will rise up against their parents and bring them to death. Disregard for the law will take hold and love among people will grow cold. — But with you, it shall not be so. Let go of your anger! You are the light of the world. Let your light shine before the people, that they may see your deeds and praise your Father in Heaven for them! Whatever you wish others to do for you, do the same for them! For what profit will a person have if he gains the whole world for himself, but suffers damage to his soul? Do not fear the Romans. Do not fear those who can kill the body but cannot kill the soul; fear the one who can destroy both body and soul! Love your enemies!

JUDAS

They are eating our crops and bread, they will devour our sons and daughters, they will swallow the sheep and cattle, they will plunder our vines and fig trees; they will destroy the cities with the sword. And we are supposed to love them?

Scene 3

NICODEMUS
Simon, we need to speak to Jesus.

SIMON OF BETHANY
What do you want from him?

JOSEPH OF ARIMATHEA
Rabbi, we know you are a great teacher. No one does signs like you, and never have I heard a person speak like you do.

NICODEMUS
In every alley of Jerusalem you can hear the words: Jesus will fight against falsehood and lead the truth to victory.

JUDAS
He speaks, but you do not accept his testimony.

NICODEMUS
Rabbi, tell us, are you the one we have been waiting for?

PETER
What are you asking? Go and report what you hear and see: The blind can see, the lame walk, the lepers are cleansed, the deaf hear and the good news is proclaimed to the poor!

LAZARUS
I was dead and lying in the pit, he called me by my name and pulled me out. Many have seen it and believe in him.

JOSEPH OF ARIMATHEA
Tell us, are you the promised one, or must we wait for someone else?

JESUS
Who do people think I am?

JOSEPH OF ARIMATHEA
Some think you are John the Baptist, because they do not want to believe that he is dead.

NICODEMUS
Or they think you are Elijah, who is to appear before the Messiah comes.

JOHN

Others believe you are Jeremiah or one of the other prophets.

JESUS

But you, who do you think I am?

(*prolonged silence*)

PETER

You are the one we have been waiting for. You are the Messiah.

JUDAS

Yes, you are the Messiah! Jesus stand up, raise your voice, lead the way, be our King.

JESUS

Judas, I will not fight nor will I shout, and my voice will not be heard in the streets.

MAGDALENE

Rabbi, upon you rests the Spirit of the LORD, the Spirit of wisdom and reason, the Spirit of counsel and strength, the Spirit of knowledge and the spirit of fear of the LORD. You do not judge by what the eyes see, nor do you judge by what the ears hear; you judge the poor and the wretched of this land with righteousness. You love truthfulness and loathe sacrilege. Grace is poured out from your lips. That is why God, your God, has anointed you before your companions. God has blessed him forever. (*Magdalene anoints him*)

THOMAS

What is she doing?

JAMES A.

She is using precious genuine nard oil.

THADDAEUS

Such an honor has never been bestowed upon our Rabbi!

JEHOSHAPHAT

Nicodemus, if this one were a prophet, he would know what kind of woman is touching him.

JESUS

Why do you think such evil in your heart? Look at this woman! She wet my feet with tears and dried them with her hair. Her sins are forgiven for she has shown so much love.

JEHOSHAPHAT

What right do you think you have? Who do you think you are to forgive sins? Who can forgive sins except for God?

JESUS

I am not doing you any wrong.

JEHOSHAPHAT

She is a whore. How can you forgive her?

JESUS

Your eyes are deluded and your heart is obdurate.

JEHOSHAPHAT

He is a talker. Let us leave!

Scene 4

JESUS

I am a worm and not a man, ridiculed and despised by everyone. All who see me deride me, open their mouths and shake their heads.

PETER

What are you talking about?

JUDAS

Why are you acting so strange!

JESUS

In the following days, all that was written by the prophets will come true in Jerusalem.

JUDAS

Rabbi! So the day has come when you will restore the kingdom of Israel?

JESUS

Peter! Andrew! James! John! Philip! Bartholomew! Thomas!

SIMON THE ZEALOT

What is happening here?

JESUS

Matthew! James Alphaeus!

JAMES A.

What is torturing you?

JESUS

Thaddaeus! Simon! Judas! Now your time has come.

— Go to the lost sheep of the house of Israel! Heal the sick, cleanse the lepers, cast out evil spirits! Freely you have received, now freely give. Speak in broad daylight of what I told you in the dark, and herald from the rooftops what I whispered in your ears! Hide nothing, everything shall be revealed.

PETER

Rabbi, you are sending us away?

JESUS

Yes, Peter! I am sending you like sheep into a pack of wolves. You will be hated by everyone. They will give you over to the courts and will beat you. You will be brought before governors and kings because of my words. But those who perseveres in their faith to the end will be saved. Therefore, do not be afraid of them!

JOHN

What are you going to do?

SIMON THE ZEALOT

What will happen?

MAGDALENE

Rabbi, do you think we do not feel it. A shadow has fallen on your face and a sorrow on your soul.

JOHN

Tell us what will happen!

JESUS

Let us go up to Jerusalem now. There I will be handed over to the Romans, they will deride me, beat me and kill me.

PETER

Kill you?

SEVERAL APOSTLES

Kill you?

JOHN

Rabbi, what dark words are you speaking to us?

PETER

God forbid! This must not happen to you! Stay in the shelter of this house until the storm that wants to rise against you has subsided!

JESUS

Away with you, Satan! Get out of my sight! You want to bring me down! You do not have in mind what God wants, but what the people want.

PETER

Rabbi! What is happening to you?

JOHN

I beg you: Do not go, lest your enemies have the opportunity to commit such atrocities!

JUDAS

Or go and reveal the power that lies within you!

JAMES Z.

Establish peace among the people!

JUDAS

I am such a fool! I thought that you would be the one who saves Israel.

ANDREAS

We left everything behind, our homes, our fields, brothers, sisters, father, mother, even our children, and followed you. What are we given in return?

THOMAS

What are we going to eat?

JAMES A.

What are we going to drink?

PHILIP

What are we going to wear?

JESUS

Those are the worries of the wicked! Seek the kingdom of God and his righteousness, and all will be given to you.

JUDAS

Really!? If you are no longer with us, our friends will soon withdraw, and then what? Rabbi, allow me, if you really want to leave us, first make arrangements for our future care!

PETER

Judas –

JUDAS

Who will provide if I do not? How much more would that pointlessly wasted oil now be worth if we still had it?!

THOMAS

The money could have been put to better use.

PETER

What are you talking about?

SIMON THE ZEALOT

Wasting such an expensive oil!

BARTHOLOMEW

What a waste!

JESUS

Why are you condemning what was done out of love? Judas, look at me!

JUDAS

Rabbi, I know you do not love pointless expenses. The oil could have been sold and the money used to support the poor. At least three hundred denarii could have been gained.

JESUS

You will always have the poor among you, but you will not always have me. She did a good deed for me. Let us leave!

MAGDALENE

Rabbi, let me go with you!

JESUS

Where I am going, you cannot follow me. — Do not let your heart be troubled! Believe in God and believe in me!

MAGDALENE

Rabbi, you are my life, Rabbi, if you leave, you take my life with you.

JESUS

Mary, if the grain of wheat does not fall into the earth and dies, it remains alone. But when it dies, it bears abundant fruit.

MAGDALENE

Rabbi, you can see: I am not crying. Strong as death is my love.

JESUS

Your love must be strong so that it does not become weak in the face of what is coming. You will search for me and wander the city, and when you find me, only your heart will recognize me, your eyes will not. For I have been thrown into the wine press, and the wine that drips out is my blood. Whatever you see, do not go mad! I am who I have always been and always will be. You have given me your love. Now also give me strength for the coming night and tomorrow!

Scene 5

(Mary, the mother of Jesus, his brothers Joseph, James, Simon and Mary Salome and Mary Cleopas appear)

MARY

Jesus!

LAZARUS

Rabbi — your mother and your brothers!

MARTHA

How fortunate we are to have our Rabbi's mother with us.

JESUS

Who is my mother, and who are my brothers?
Everyone who fulfills my Father's will is a brother and a sister and a mother to me!

MARY

Jesus, I have been anxiously looking for you.

JESUS

Why were you looking for me? You knew where I was.

MARY

Yes, I knew. Oh son, how can I understand you? Your fervor for your father's house is consuming you. Come back to Nazareth!

BROTHER JAMES

When are you going to give up your roaming? You itinerant preacher!

BROTHER SIMON

What do you actually live on? From charity or from the money of those women there!? Shame!

BROTHER JOSEPH

You preach the commandments to others, but you yourself do not even know the fourth: You shall honor your father and mother! Are you taking care of your mother?

BROTHER SIMON

And not only that! You also take away the sons of other families and make vagabonds out of honest fishermen and craftsmen, you prevent them from starting their own family and becoming respectable citizens. Where does all this lead to?

BROTHER JAMES

They say you give speeches against the powerful — that will turn out badly for you.

JESUS

James, blessed are those who hear and follow the Word of God!

BROTHER JOSEPH

Come with us now and see reason!

MARY

Leave him be! He must follow his own path.

JESUS

Do not worry, Mother! Do not worry!

MARY

What do you mean, I should not worry about you? Are you not in my prayers, day and night? You have outgrown my hands, in which I carried you, but my soul, holds on to you...and it watches over your life.

LAZARUS

Mary, he is going to Jerusalem! His enemies lie in wait for his downfall.

MARY

To Jerusalem! I once carried you in my arms to the temple there, to bring you to the Lord! The Lord gave you to me, now he is reclaiming you. What He imposes on me, I will endure! My son. Where will I see you again?

JESUS

Where the words of the Scripture are fulfilled: „He was like a lamb that is led to the slaughter and opens not its mouth."

MARY

Lord, give me strength that my heart may not break!

JESUS

Mother, you will weep and wail. You will be sad, but your sadness shall be turned into joy, and your joy no one shall take from you. Let us go.

THE GOLDEN CALF

CHOIR

„O golden image! We kneel down before you!
You great ruler! You, our guardian!
We thank the one, who frees us from Egypt!
O strong helper, help us always!
You golden god!
Who sets us free!
You helped in time of need!
Help us today, too!
Lead us forward!
We worship you!
You always give us your faithful guidance!
Splendor you will give! Glory!
Come, let us dance around him with strings!
Come, we want to please him with our dance!
Since we have been left by Moses and his God,
You be our protector and shield in all distress!
Who else but you helps us, helps us in life and death?!
You golden image! You strong God!
Filled with reverence we stand here!
O golden God! See, your people,
They plead to you!"

BASS — SOLO

How I shudder at the sins of the people!
From whom? From whom, you unfaithful, do you
seek counsel?!
Was it not Yahweh who led you at all times
Do you not consider the abyss?
Satan's power will arise anew!
Show this false god his vision of night!

„Let me lead you to the Father!"
Jesus lovingly invites all,
The good shepherd does not want to lose a sheep!
Judas should also be with him there!
Alas, Judas wants to let go of Jesus,

his heavenly kingdom he cannot grasp,
confides himself to the enemy lines,
and they demand, O holy God,
to punish Jesus with death!

CHOIR

Turn back, all of you, from the path of sin!
Entrust yourselves to the Father!
For behold, through false gods deaf and blind
people fall into the path of destruction,
the heart grows cold and freezes to death,
when it loses its bond with God.

EXPULSION OF THE MERCHANTS FROM THE TEMPLE PILATE AND CAIAPHAS

Scene 1

DATHAN

He is coming! He is coming!

JESUS

Listen to me! Thus says the LORD, the God of Israel:
Improve your ways and your deeds, and I will let you
live in this place, in the land I gave to your ancestors
before generations, to be theirs forever.

NATHANAEL

What are you bothering these people for?

JESUS

Is this a house of God — or is it a marketplace? The
children of Israel that come to Jerusalem for the
Passover to worship God. Can they perform their
prayers in this turmoil?

EZEKIEL

All this is intended as offering to the Lord.

JESUS

If you only knew what that meant: I am pleased
by mercy and not by sacrifice. Did God command
sacrifices on the day He brought our fathers out of
Egypt?

NATHANAEL

Yes.

JESUS

No! He commanded you: Do as I say, and I will be
your God, and you will be my people. Walk the path
the LORD commands you! —

ARCHELAUS

You dare to exhort us, the priests?

JESUS

Hear, Israel! The LORD our God is the LORD alone!
Love him, with all your heart, with all your mind and
with all your strength! No other commandment is
more important.

NICODEMUS

He is right.

NATHANAEL

Nicodemus!

NICODEMUS

There is only One and none other but Him! To love
the LORD with all your heart, with all your mind,
and with all your strength, and to love your neighbor
as you love yourself, is worth more than all burnt
offerings and sacrifices.

JESUS

Nicodemus, you are not far from the kingdom of God.
— (to the merchants) Leave! Go away! There is enough
space outside the temple for your business.

BOOZ

So, we are not allowed to make sacrifices anymore?

ALBION

How can you forbid what the High Council allows us
to do?

JESUS

„My house," says the Lord, „shall be called a house of

prayer for all nations." But you have made it a den of thieves. And you, priests, guardians of the sanctuary, why do you look upon these atrocities and tolerate them?

ARCHELAUS

The Lord spoke: Whoever wants to offer a sacrifice among you, let him bring it to the entrance of the temple, that he may please the LORD.

NATHANAEL

You, deluded people, you want to follow this innovator? Do not listen to him! He has come to repeal the law.

JESUS

I have not come to repeal the law or remove the prophets! I have not come to abolish, but to fulfill.

EZEKIEL

Enough! Away now, from the steps of the temple! Only Yahweh's messenger, the priests and the scribes are permitted on these sacred steps! We alone are allowed to proclaim God's will!

NATHANAEL

Do not listen to him! Woe to the man who tempts to do evil! Free yourselves from the shackles of his words!

ARCHELAUS

Do you want to abandon Moses, the prophets and his priests?!

PETER

No! We do not want that! Far be it from us to forsake Moses and his law.

ANNAS

But who has the right to proclaim God's law to you? Who is entrusted with the duty of protecting doctrinal purity? Is it not the priests and teachers?

ARCHELAUS

So who do you want to listen to? To us or to this seducer who has proclaimed himself the herald of a new doctrine?

PHILIP

He is a great prophet!

PETER

He is the Messiah!

ARCHELAUS

He is a false teacher!

EZEKIEL

An enemy of Moses!

ARCHELAUS

An enemy of the statutes of our fathers!

ANNAS

Disobedience is a sin as evil as sorcery, and reluctance is like idolatry and worshipping a false god. Only we, your fathers, will save you from the abyss.

JESUS

The scribes and priests have sat down on Moses' chair. Everything they tell you, do and abide by it!

NATHANAEL

Hear, hear! He is inclined to follow his lawful authorities.

JESUS

But do not follow their deeds! For they talk, but do not practice what they preach.

ISHMAEL

How dare you?

JESUS

They bind heavy and unbearable burdens and impose them on your shoulders, but they themselves will not lift a finger. Everything they do, they only do to be seen by the people; their prayer cords have wide straps and their tassels are long. They value the place of honor at banquets and the seat of honor in synagogues and want to be greeted in the marketplaces and called rabbi by everyone.

ARCHELAUS

Who are you that you dare to revile the priests with such speech?

JESUS

You do not want to listen, you only follow your own

advice and your obdurate hearts. But to the LORD
you turn your back and not your face.

NATHANAEL

Enough! You listen to words of lies that serve no
purpose. Cast off the yoke of the seducer!

AMMIEL

Follow the High Council!

NATHANAEL

Children of Israel! Do you want to stop being God's
chosen people?

JESUS

You hypocrites, woe to you who close the gates of the
kingdom of heaven for the people! You do not enter,
and those who want to, you do not let in. Woe to you
who traverse land and sea to win one over to your
faith; and when he believes, you make him a child of
hell twice as evil as you are.

EZEKIEL

Enough!

NATHANAEL

Throw him out!

ISHMAEL

Expel him from the temple!

COUNCILORS

Silence ... Traitor ... your loyalty bought... who are you
... down with him... who are you...

JESUS

You deluded leaders, you devour the houses of widows
and perform long prayers for the sake of appearances.
You are just like the obscure tombs that look beautiful
on the outside, but inside they are full of dry bones
and filth! On the outside you seem pious to everyone,
but on the inside you are full of hypocrisy and
contempt for the law. Woe to you who give a tenth
of mint, dill and caraway and leave aside the most
important thing in the Law, namely, justice, mercy
and faith! — *(To the merchants)* Away from here — I
command you! Take what is yours and leave this holy
place!

ALBION

This is unacceptable!

JESUS

Out with all of it!

EPHOD

You cannot do that!

KOSAM

My money!

ESROM

My pigeons!

BOOZ

My sheep!

EPHOD

My jars of oil spilled! Who will compensate me for the damage?

JESUS

Away with you! I want this desecrated place to be given back to the worship of the Father.

JUDAS

Shma Israel....

PEOPLE

Shma Israel, Adonaj Elohejnu, Adonaj Echad. Baruch schem kwod malchuto le'olam wa'ed. We'ahawta et Adonaj Elohecha, bechol lewawcha, uwechol nafschecha, uwechol meodecha! Shma Israel!

JESUS

Be firm in your faith. You can see it. God Himself has brought it before your eyes, and although you recognize God, you do not give Him the glory He is due. Your thoughts get lost in the void and your ignorant heart darkens.

SOME

The Romans! (The people run away)

Scene 2

LONGINUS

What the devil is going on here? Go back to your homes! Priests! What is the meaning of this turmoil? Clamor and uproar in every alley!

NATHANAEL

He came.

LONGINUS

Who came?

ARCHELAUS

The Galilean.

LONGINUS

Who? His name!

NATHANAEL

Jesus, the son of a carpenter from Nazareth ...

LONGINUS

Whose son? What do you know about him? Who is he?

PETER

He is the great prophet from Nazareth.

JUDAS

Praise him who comes in the name of the Lord!

JOHN

Hosanna!

PEOPLE AND CHILDREN

Hosanna to the Son of David!

LONGINUS

You and your followers — leave! I do not want any trouble!

PETER

Leave him be! There will be no trouble!

A ROMAN

The pig is talking back! *(Pilate appears with an entourage)*

LONGINUS

The fellow rebels, against a man of the emperor. Throw him into the mud!

OTHER ROMANS

Take this, — and this!

45

LONGINUS

Tan their goddamned skins! Now leave! Leave!

NATHANAEL

Governor of the noble emperor!

PRIESTS

Every blessing to you!

PILATE

I want to talk to the high priest.

CAIAPHAS

Pilate

PILATE

Alone!

LONGINUS

Are you deaf? Alone!

PILATE

(To Caiaphas) There is a great upheaval in the city.
Caiaphas, did anything special happen here?

CAIAPHAS

Many pilgrims come to Jerusalem for the Passover ...

PILATE

Many pilgrims ... I see ...you know what I mean.

CAIAPHAS

Yes. Pilate, he is an insignificant itinerant preacher —

PILATE

Insignificant? Well, well! The whole city comes out
to meet him. He entered Jerusalem like a king. You,
the priests and teachers, have become the plaything
of a man who defies you and ridicules you. And you
call that insignificant? Caiaphas, let me enlighten you.
It is precisely these insignificant itinerant preachers
who, under the pretext of divine mission, provoke
revolution and turmoil and tempt the people to fall
into religious dedication. They lure them into the
desert, as if your God were to announce their freedom
there by miraculous signs, and then ... then?
(Caiaphas stays silent)

LONGINUS

Admiration, it seems, has left you speechless.

CAIAPHAS

The city is quiet. No one is looking for turmoil or
revolution.

PILATE

No one? I know you Jews. What purpose did your
people serve before I took them over? A lost bunch —
without obedience, without leadership. I offered you
Jews peace, freedom and an amnesty for your crimes,
but you disdained my gifts and only after I ordered a
horde of rebels to be crucified and those who made
common cause with them be executed was there peace
in this godforsaken land.

CAIAPHAS

Pilate. I beg you.

PILATE

You beg me? I allowed you to stay high priest, I gave
you the office to watch over the peace and order in
this city, I gave you everything you begged me for. *(to
his soldiers)* I gave it to him because the hand of his
God, was over him. *(laughs)*

CAIAPHAS

You are mocking me.

PILATE

No, I am not mocking you. If there is no peace in the
city, I will take away everything I gave you. You know
the emperor's message to all the governors of the
empire.

CAIAPHAS

I know his message.

PILATE

Then you also know how his message ends: If there
is conflict in the land and rebellion against Rome, I
will come with military forces and bring destruction
to you, your land and your people. Now go! Throw
this Galilean into the dungeon, and if he is not
understanding even then....

CAIAPHAS

... then? Pilate, do you want me to kill him?

PILATE

I never want to hear about this Jesus again. Not ever again!

CAIAPHAS

You know his name?

PILATE

I know him!

LONGINUS

The governor is very well informed about all activities and actions of the Jews.

PILATE

Did he not say: I will set you free? And — do you believe him? *(laughs)* You will come to understand that you will never be free. Your people, Caiaphas, are weak, vicious and insignificant. Go now! I am glad that you are so happy to comply! And, Caiaphas — whatever happens, do not forget that you can count on my soldiers!

(Pilate with entourage departing)

IV. PRESENTATION
THE RED SEA

CHOIR

> Flee! Flee! Egypt's army is approaching with might!
> Where to? Where to can we flee? Before us the sea's shore!
> No path! No bridge! The sea foretelling our impending doom!
> We are lost! All paths are blocked!

TENOR — SOLO

> Do not be afraid of the Pharaoh's might!
> Hidden in clouds and fire
> Yahweh will save you soon —
> He, his people's liberator!

SOLOISTS

> And Moses extended his hand,
> the waters swept away by the east wind,
> and Israel's people travelled over dry land
> between walls of water that still would stand.

CHOIR

> Great things the Lord has done,
> He leads Israel on a safe path!
> When You guide us on unknown paths,
> let us believe in Your grace!
> If Your goals we cannot see,
> let our trust in You set us free!

THE HIGH COUNCIL
JUDAS AND CAIAPHAS

Scene 1

CAIAPHAS

> Woe to the children of Israel! Woe to the holy city!
> Woe to the temple of the Lord! And woe to me if I put
> up with his provoking demeanor and arrogant speech!

NATHANAEL

Calm down. This Roman mocker is like a dog that in his ignorance barks at the moon!

ARCHELAUS

And all this because of some arbitrary Galilean!

ANNAS

The people turn their backs on us and the whole world is running after him.

EZEKIEL

The number of his followers grows endlessly.

JOSEPH OF ARIMATHEA

Are you surprised?

CAIAPHAS

Joseph, what are you saying?

JOSEPH OF ARIMATHEA

Caiaphas, you have been chosen to represent the people before God, it is your duty to prevent harm to the people. They hope for freedom, but nothing good comes their way; they hope for salvation, but there is terror in the land.

CAIAPHAS

Joseph, we know that you do not seek worldly wealth, that you act prudently and to the best of your knowledge, you are humble, many of the elders trust in your word and show you respect. But you have no idea of what is going on here.

JOSEPH OF ARIMATHEA

Then explain it to me.

EZEKIEL

What is there to explain! He derides and disrespects us! With every passing day he becomes more dangerous.

ANNAS

Caiaphas! Speak! Why have you not imprisoned him yet? We have become the people's laughing stock.

EZEKIEL

Every time he opens his mouth, he defies and derides us.

NICODEMUS

Our land lies in ruins, our cities burnt down; strangers waste the fields before our very eyes; all has been destroyed, ravaged by the Romans. But you close your eyes to the poverty of the people. You surround yourselves with the hated Romans and do not understand that the people condemn us for it.

CAIAPHAS

What? Are we supposed to accept his disparagement of us, the priests and teachers, calling us hypocrites and blind guides? How are we supposed to tolerate him deceiving the people and spreading a false doctrine that undermines the law? Nicodemus, how are we supposed tolerate how he irritates the Romans and thus puts us, the whole city and the temple in danger.

NICODEMUS

It is our fault that it has come to this. We deal in lies and only heal the people's pain on the surface, preaching „Peace! Peace!" Yet, there is no peace.

JOSEPH OF ARIMATHEA

Look around you! The city is full of people who have left their homes because the drought has destroyed their seedlings and laid waste to their vineyards and oil gardens. There they lie — men, women and children — in great numbers, along the walls of the houses, famine growling in their stomachs. But what do we have to offer them? Peace!?

SIMON OF BETHANY

We stand there in disgrace, because we kept silent about the atrocities.

NATHANAEL

Nicodemus is right! It is our fault that it has come to this, ours — because of our hesitation! Joseph, what good did it do to try to embarrass the Galilean by asking him questions, to prove to him his deviations from the teachings of our fathers, his violations of the law? Nothing! The people turn their backs on us and the whole world is running after him. We are responsible for this, friends and brothers, we, the guardians of Zion!

JOSEPH OF ARIMATHEA

Then take the responsibility upon yourself!

ANNAS

What are you talking about, Joseph? To our shame,
we had to witness the Galilean and his followers
pass through the gates and through the streets of
our holy city. You yourself heard how the besotted
masses shouted „Hosanna!". With your own eyes you
witnessed how that arrogant man claimed the seat of
the high priest for himself and dared to judge us as the
lord in the temple of God. How much time is left until
the complete upheaval of all state and divine order?

ARCHELAUS

It was not enough that he entered our city with a
crowd of cheering people behind him! Using a whip,
he dared to drive out the merchants in the atrium of
the temple who were offering the goods necessary for
sacrifice.

GERSHON

Money, oil, salt, pigeons — he has to replace
everything!

SIMON OF BETHANY

Brothers! Those who are discontent are rising up.
They are calling for a king on David's throne. But us
they accuse of playing into the hands of the Romans.

NATHANAEL

If you, Caiaphas, do not intervene, the people's
resentment will turn against you.

EZEKIEL

Against you and against us!

ANNAS

How much longer are you going to hesitate before
putting an end to this stream of perdition? All the
dams have already been breached, and like an all-
destructive flood, the wildly gushing wave has rolled
over all of Judea. The foundation walls have been
flooded, and in the blink of an eye, we will be buried
under the wreckage of the collapsing building.

NATHANAEL

(To Caiaphas) One more step, and the law that God gave us through Moses will be overthrown, the teachings condemned, the priests stripped of their titles!

CAIAPHAS

Patience, friends!

NATHANAEL

I implore you, High Priest!

CAIAPHAS

Patience! He has too many followers.

JOSEPH OF ARIMATHEA

Caiaphas, listen to me!

CAIAPHAS

What do you want Joseph?

JOSEPH OF ARIMATHEA

To speak to your heart and to your conscience.

CAIAPHAS

To my heart?

JOSEPH OF ARIMATHEA

The people are turning their backs on us. Why would they believe our words?

CAIAPHAS

For the sake of our friendship, be silent!

JOSEPH OF ARIMATHEA

I stand before my High Priest with reverence; but I will not be silent. Far be it from me to defend what this Jesus has said in his excessive fervor. But he did it for the cause of God.

NATHANAEL

What are you talking about?

ANNAS

Are you out of your mind?

JOSEPH OF ARIMATHEA

He does not judge by what his eyes see, nor does he judge by what his ears hear; he judges the poor and wretched of the land with righteousness. But what do we do? We enjoy being greeted in the synagogues and in the market and being called "Rabbi" by the people.

Our prayer cords have wide straps and the tassels on our clothes are long.

ANNAS

Have you never read: You shall make holy garments for Aaron, for glory and beauty!

NICODEMUS

Yes, that is what we were given by Moses. But there it is also written: Pride goes before a fall!

EZEKIEL

Nicodemus!

NICODEMUS

With all our actions we try to catch the wind.

SIMON OF BETHANY

Nicodemus, do not be so quick with your words.

NICODEMUS

I dislike those who are arrogant and proud.

NATHANAEL

He has been a secret follower of the Galilean for a long time! Now he has revealed his true colors!

JOSEPH OF ARIMATHEA

Brothers, many have turned their backs on us; but his words have ignited the light of the Lord in many of those with a cold heart.

NICODEMUS

Are you really surprised that our brothers long to rise against the misery that has befallen them? They long for the light. Caiaphas, we cannot allow this Jesus to proclaim himself as king of Israel. We cannot allow the hated Roman to be irritated by him. But do not condemn him for his words!

ANNAS

You will live in shame because of what you are saying.

NATHANAEL

They know nothing about shame. Look, look! You can see the madness burning in his eyes.

CAIAPHAS

Call it madness. But it is more than that. It is admiration for the Galilean.

ANNAS

The seducer has reached our ranks with his nets.

EZEKIEL

Thus, we have followers of the Galilean even among ourselves.

AMMIEL

We must put an end to the activities of this teacher of false doctrines.

JEHOSHAPHAT

We must decide today what has to be done.

CAIAPHAS

Believe me, Nicodemus, no one shall be persecuted for their words. But do I have the right to stop him after everything he has made himself guilty of? Joseph, how am I supposed to go on hoping for happiness for our people if I let him continue with his work? I command you to be silent from now on and to never speak the name of the Galilean again.

JOSEPH OF ARIMATHEA

So I have to choose between fearing you and obeying God?

NICODEMUS

You command us? Now you can see how far the Roman's arm reaches.

CAIAPHAS

The Roman's arm is powerful, but I do not tremble before his might. Listen to me: This dreamer recklessly brings our city into turmoil. He turns the law into an ungodly doctrine. But where there is no law, the people become wild and disobedient! Blessed are those who maintain order! Encouraged by his success, the Galilean will proclaim himself the king of Israel. You know what happens then! If there is to be peace while this Nazarene preaches, we have to do what should have been done long ago now and without hesitation. We must —

ARCHELAUS

We must throw him into prison, simply put: render him harmless.

JEHOSHAPHAT

This will make the proper impression on his followers and cool their dedication to him when he, who has promised them freedom, himself lies in chains.

GERSHON

Into the deepest dungeon with him! There he shall be put and there he shall stay, buried alive!

CAIAPHAS

But which of you wants to ensure that the guards will not be bribed into letting him escape? Or that he will not use his magic skills to break the shackles and open the dungeon door? Or that his friends will not instigate a riot in order to free him? Who among you dares to guarantee that? *(All are silent)* I can see clearly: no one. Then go!

NATHANAEL

Caiaphas?

CAIAPHAS

Go away! I alone will decide what to do!

Scene 2

DATHAN

What are you going to do?

SELPHA

He comes to the temple every day, there he can be captured.

CAIAPHAS

No. To catch him now during the Passover festivities is too dangerous. We cannot dare to capture him — not in the temple nor on the open streets, because he is always surrounded by a crowd of enthusiastic followers.

DATHAN

Shall we sit quietly and wait until after the festivities?

SELPHA

It has to happen now.

DATHAN

The matter does not allow any kind of delay.

CAIAPHAS

We must not take him with open force. We must try to capture him secretly.

JUDAS

Caiaphas!

SELPHA

Who are you?

JUDAS

Caiaphas! You are looking for Jesus of Nazareth.

SELPHA

Who are you?

JUDAS

What do you want from him?

CAIAPHAS

Do you know this man?

JUDAS

Yes. I know him.

DATHAN

He is one of the follower of the Galilean. I saw him many times with him.

SELPHA

Take him!

CAIAPHAS

Selpha! What is your name?

JUDAS

My name is Judas. From Iscariot

CAIAPHAS

Speak! What do you want?

JUDAS

I overheard the priests in the atrium. They say you want to capture him.

CAIAPHAS

Who says such absurd nonsense? Is it not written: You shall not take vengeance, nor bear any grudge against the children of your people. —

SERVANT OF CAIAPHAS

Leviticus 19: 18

CAIAPHAS

You are right! - Judas, what is it about him? Why are you a disciple of the Galilean?

JUDAS

I followed him, because I wanted to live a righteous life.

CAIAPHAS

Your rabbi speaks harshly against us and disregards the advice given to him by the elders. Judas, I can see resentment in your eyes.

JUDAS

Only against myself!

CAIAPHAS

Speak! What is it?

JUDAS

Lately, I have been tormented by disturbing thoughts...

CAIAPHAS

What kind of thoughts? Tell us! How else can we trust you?

JUDAS

I worship him. In his eyes burns a great light. All my hopes rest on him. Every day, every night I told myself: He will be great and the Lord will give him the throne of his father David, and he will be king over the house of Jacob forever, and his kingdom will have no end.

CAIAPHAS

Your thoughts frighten me, they are dangerous. Make sure that no Roman ever hears them. They have ears in every corner of the city.

JUDAS

I had hoped he would wipe the tears from our faces and end the humiliation the Romans are bringing on our people.

CAIAPHAS

And now? Are you doubting him?

JUDAS

I do not want to talk about it.

CAIAPHAS

Judas, you cannot know how things will stand with me — have no fear. I loathe the Romans just like you! — I admire your rabbi. That is why I want to speak to him — and that is the only reason why I am looking for him. I am searching for him like a shepherd searches for his sheep when they stray from his flock. — You know where he resides in the evening. Would you be willing to show us the location of his whereabouts?

JUDAS

No.

CAIAPHAS

Judas, have faith! In the silence and seclusion of the night lead him to me and no one shall ever know anything about it.

DATHAN

Judas, you can still become a respected and wealthy man.

CAIAPHAS

Judas, it might be advisable for some of my men to accompany you.

SELPHA

At nightfall I will be waiting for you at the gate of Bethpage. *(Judas departs)*

CAIAPHAS

He will come.

DATHAN

You chirp like a swallow and coo like a dove.

CAIAPHAS

The matter is turning out exactly as desired. Soon, Jesus of Nazareth will be in our hands.

THE BURNING BUSH

CHOIR

> From the thorn's radiant embers,
> and a flood of blazing flames
> Moses hears on mount Horeb's holy place
> his God's pressing command:

SECOND CHOIR

> „Moses, go stand before the Pharaoh's throne!
> In my name end Israel's servitude!"

TENOR — SOLO

> „Who am I to speak to the Pharaoh?
> You know my powerlessness, my weakness!"

SECOND CHOIR

> „Listen, Moses! For the sake of Israel
> you shall fulfill my behest!"

TENOR — SOLO

> „Lord, send another in my stead!"

SECOND CHOIR

> „I will be with you! Follow my command!"

CHOIR

> And so the Lord from the flaming thorn sends
> Moses away in holy wrath.
> And Jesus prays as well: „Let the cup of death pass me!
> Yet, not my will, Father,
> but only yours be done!"

CONTRALTO — SOLO

> I heard Israel's plea,
> I saw your tribulation,
> your suffering, your tears,
> your sorrow, your yearning!
> Everything you suffered, I have suffered with you.

Your sorrows I will turn to joy!
I will wrest you from the clutches of the enemy!
I will watch over you,
I will show you the way
to your land this very night.

CHOIR

May His mercy last forever
He, who set us free!
Who brought back Jesus from the dead,
who is with us in fear and dread,
whose hand holds us,
where evil surrounds us,
everlasting be His grace!
and His mercy keep us safe!

THE LAST SUPPER

Scene 1

JOHN

Why are you standing so afar and hiding your face?

JESUS

Jerusalem, you may yet realize it. How often have I
tried to gather your children, like a hen gathers her
chicks under her wings, and you refused!
It is like in the days of Noah, in the days before the
Flood — they ate, they drank, they married and were
given in marriage, until the day Noah entered his ark,
but they did not care, the Flood came and swept them
all away. Be wary, for you do not know on what day
the Lord is coming! Be ready! For He will come when
you do not expect Him.

THOMAS

Rabbi, your enemies speak evil of you.

PETER

You have worked signs before the people — and yet
they do not follow you.

JAMES

Who believes the words you preach?

THADDAEUS

They look but still do not see. They hear but still do
not listen or understand it.

BARTHOLOMEW

The heart of the people is stubborn.

JOHN

Mockery comes from their lips and derision from
their gaze.

JAMES A.

Who trusts in God's power?

PETER

They come in droves to see you, and yet they do not
come with sincere hearts; but rather are looking for
something to gossip about, then they leave and carry
it out into the streets.

THADDAEUS

Heathens they are and blind!

JESUS

The light has come into the world, but people love the
darkness more than the light.

JUDAS

I hoped for light, and darkness arrived. — Life is given
to us so we can offer it to God and His Spirit. I want to
offer myself, I want to die for Israel and His reign on
earth.

JESUS

Judas, seek peace, seek peace. Do not turn to those
who sit in darkness, in the shadow of death, and set
your feet on the path for peace.

JUDAS

My soul has forgotten the meaning of peace; and I
have forgotten what happiness is!

PETER

We are strangers to each other like the trees of the

forest, yet they grow quietly next to each other, while we rage against each other with axe and spear until the blood pours out of our bodies. What is it that brings death amongst humanity and sows hatred between us? I do not understand it!

THOMAS

Rabbi, why does God allow this to happen?

JOHN

What are you talking about? God does not wish for these sacrileges. We make him responsible for all that we do not understand.

JUDAS

Did God not say: „Take vengeance on the Midianites for what they did to the Israelites"? God wants us to fight back! God wants —

PETER

Judas, detach the name of God from war, for it is not God who wages war, but people! No war is sacred, no death is sacred, only life is sacred.

JESUS

Those who want peace are in eternal conflict. The gentle must be strong. Blessed are those who are persecuted for righteousness.

JUDAS

Who can listen to this? Why should I continue to follow you? I have little desire to do so. Your great deeds gave hope that you would restore the kingdom of Israel. But it will come to nothing, you are not seizing the opportunity that presents itself to you. Now you speak of parting and dying and try to console us with mysterious words and a future that is too dark and far removed for my taste.

PETER

Judas!

JUDAS

Rabbi, I worship you, but I am tired of believing and hoping.

SIMON THE ZEALOT

My hope in the LORD is also forsaken.

JUDAS

There is nothing to expect for our future but perpetual poverty and lowliness, and instead of the rule over your kingdom, only persecution and imprisonment. Your governance I wanted to share with you. But it is nowhere to be seen. And what is visible — horror and misery — who would want to be a part of that? Not me! Not me!

JESUS

Then leave! If you follow me, you will be outcasts; if you follow me, you will be hated. Blessed are you when people vilify you because of me and speak evil against you. Why are you sad? Why are you looking at me with such worry? Be happy! You have eyes and see. You have ears and hear. Many prophets, many righteous and pious people desired to see what you see, to hear what you hear.

JOHN

I will go with you!

SIMON THE ZEALOT

Me too.

PETER

Rabbi, where you go, I will also go.

JESUS

Come! I earnestly wish to celebrate the Passover meal with you.

(Takes a basin of water)

ANDREAS

What do you want to do? What are you doing?

PETER

Rabbi, you want to wash my feet? No, Lord, you shall never wash my feet.

JESUS

You call me Lord and Rabbi. But a lord is not greater than the slave. You know, that rulers oppress their people and the powerful abuse the weak. It shall not be so with you; whoever wishes to be great among you, let him be your servant; and whoever wishes to be first among you, let him be your slave.

PETER

> Rabbi, not only wash my feet, then, but also my hands
> and my head!
>
> *(begins to wash their feet)*

JESUS

> I am among you as a servant. Follow me and act as I
> do towards you!
>
> *(All are silent and Thomas lights the candle)*

THOMAS

> Blessed is the match that is consumed in kindling
> flame.

JOHN

> Blessed is the flame that burns in the secret fastness of
> the heart!

THOMAS

> Blessed is the heart with the strength to stop its
> beating for honor's sake.

PETER

> May our hearts be risen up, our souls invigorated,
> when we kindle the light.

JOHN

> Barúch attá adonáj elohénu.

ALL APOSTLES

> Mélech haolám, aschér kiddeschánu bemizvotáv
> weziwwánu lehadlík ner schel yom tov.

PETER

> Praise be to you, our God, who sanctified the people
> of Israel!

JOHN

> What makes this night different from all other nights?

PETER

> On this night the Lord led Israel out of Egypt with a
> strong hand and a raised arm.

ANDREAS

> He divided the Red Sea in two, led Israel through
> between the wall of water.

JUDAS

> He led his people through the desert, gave the land as
> heritage to the children Israel, his servants.

JOHN

This is the day that the Lord has made.

JESUS

Our Father in heaven, hallowed be your name, your Kingdom come.

PHILIP

Your will be done on earth, as it is in heaven!

THADDAEUS

Give us the daily bread we need!

MATTHEW

Forgive us our sins, as we forgive those who sin against us!

PETER

Lead us when there is temptation and save us from evil!

JESUS

Baruch attá, adonáj elohénu, mélech haolám, hamozí léchem min haárez. — *(Breaks the bread and gives it to them)*

Our fathers ate manna in the desert and died. Those who come to God will never be hungry, and those who believe in Him will never be thirsty. Whoever eats of this bread will live forever.

Take some! Eat! Whenever you break this bread, do so in remembrance of me.

(Takes the cup) Baruch attá, adonáj elohénu, mélech haolám boray pri hagafen. Blessed are you, Adonai our God, Ruler of the Universe, creator of the fruit of the vine! He who believes in God, from his body rivers of living water will flow. Drink! *(Gives them the cup)* This is my commandment, love one another as I have loved you.

ANGEL

Jerusalem, put on the garment of sorrow! Weep, you people on Mount Zion!

Agony and abyss will be granted to him, pain and persecution. He endures every disgrace he is confronted with, and offers his cheek to the one who strikes him. The people ridicule him, he is the target of their mockery by day and night.

JESUS

Friend, whatever you are about to do, do it quickly!
(Judas leaves the room.)

JOHN

Why is Judas leaving?

JESUS

It would be better for him if he had never been born.

SOPRANO — SOLO

See Jesus kneeling in the olive grove,
dying of sorrow,
and with tears in his eyes and crying out loud
he surrenders himself to the father!

CHOIR

So, you all want to go with Jesus,
watch him suffer, endure, die!

JESUS ON THE MOUNT OF OLIVES

Scene 1

JOHN

So, the hour has come when you will be surrendered into the hands of your enemies?

PETER

Rabbi, can nothing stop you?

JESUS

Simon, I want the world to see that I love God and act as He has instructed me.

JOHN

They are going to kill you.

THOMAS

(to John) He who raises the dead cannot die.

JAMES A.

What can your enemies do to you —

ANDREAS

A word from you could crush them all!

JAMES Z.

The Lord will preserve you and keep your life and will not give you up to the will of your enemies.

(Jesus is silent)

JOHN

Stay with us, Rabbi!

JESUS

What can I say: Father, save me from this hour!? I was born into the world because of this hour.

PETER

Rabbi, where you go, I will also go.

JESUS

Where I am going, you cannot follow now. But you will follow me later.

PHILIP

I have never seen him so disheartened.

JESUS

Tonight, you will all be angry with me.

PETER

Even if everyone is angry with you, I will never.

JESUS

The Lord will strike the shepherd, and his sheep will scatter. Peter, before the cock crows, you will deny me three times.

PETER

Lord, I am willing to go to prison with you. And if I had to die with you, I will never deny you.

JESUS

Simon, Simon, Satan has desired to sift you like wheat. I have prayed for you that your faith may not fail. Strengthen your brothers! Stay here and keep vigil with me!

JOHN

My soul suffers with yours.

JESUS

I have become a stranger to my brothers. I am only devoted to You, my God since I was in my mother's womb. Father, You loved me before the world had been created. When I was still in my mother's womb, You named me. You made my mouth a sharp sword. Father, I have preached Your will to the people, I have given them Your word, but the world hated it.

ANGEL

For the sake of Israel, my chosen people, I have called you by your name. I placed my spirit upon you to free all those that live in darkness from their imprisonment.

JESUS

The world did not recognized you, but I did. My strength has dried up like a shard. My tongue sticks to my palate. My soul is dying of sorrow. Everything is darkening around me now! The fear of death envelops me. Simon! — (*Turns to the disciples*)

PETER

Rabbi! Rabbi!

JESUS

Could you keep vigil with me for an hour?

PETER

Forgive me! I will keep vigil with you.

James

Sleep has overwhelmed me.

JOHN

Rabbi, we will keep vigil and pray with you.

ANGEL

Through you I will show my glory. I will make you the light for the people, so that my salvation may reach every corner of the earth.

JESUS

You lay me in the dust of death. May the depths not swallow me up, may the hole of the pit not close up over me! Father, stay near to me! Father! The gates of heaven will be opened. The foundations of earth will be shaken. The earth will shatter. The sins of the people weigh on her. Save me, Father, do not hide Your face from me! Father! Do not leave me! My Father! Father! Your son!

ANGEL

Rise up! The hour of darkness is nigh. Carry the sickness of the people! Take the pain upon yourself! Let yourself be pierced by their crimes, crushed by their sins! Heal them through your wounds!

JESUS

If it is possible, let this cup of darkness pass me by! But if it is not possible for this hour to pass me by, Your will be done! I will not retreat, will not hide my face from abuse or spit. Yes, Father, Your will be done!

Scene 2

PETER

What is the meaning of this turmoil? Rabbi!

ANDREAS

What does this horde want?

JOHN

Look! Judas is leading them!

JUDAS

Greetings, Rabbi!

JESUS

Friend, you came. *(To the soldiers)* Who are you looking for?

HORDE

Jesus of Nazareth!

JESUS

That is me. You have come to fight me as you would against a robber with swords and with truncheons. I sat with you every day in the temple and taught you, and you did not reach out your hand for me or take hold of me. Yet, this is your hour, this the power of darkness. Look, here I am!

SELPHA

Take him!

JOHN

Lord, cast them down that they may never rise again! *(Peter strikes Malchus with his sword. Malchus screams)*

JESUS

Peter Those who wield the sword will perish by the sword!

MALCHUS

My ear, I am wounded!

JESUS

(Touches the ear of Malchus) Do not worry! — I have told you who I am. So if you are looking for me, let the others go!

SELPHA

Take him! Tie him up so that he cannot escape!

NATHANAEL

You will have to answer to the High Council for this.

BALBUS

He will not be able to break free from our hold.

MELCHI

You shall pay dearly for your sacrileges.

CHOIR

Started has the battle of pain,
started in Gethsemani.
O sinners, take it to your hearts,
never forget this incident!
This happened for your salvation,
what you saw on the Mount of Olives.

SOPRANO / CONTRALTO — DUET

For us Jesus is already willing,
to give himself over to death,
for us he drinks the cup of bitterness,
for our salvation, that we may live.
Look, O human, the shackles on his hands
are his sacrifice for your freedom!

End of the first part of the Passion Play

THE PROPHET DANIEL IN THE LION'S DEN

CONTRALTO — SOLO

My heart is bleeding!
The saint is on trial —
he must bear violence and malevolence,
betrayed and insulted, chained and beaten!
No disciple wants to pledge their allegiance to him
anymore!
Carried to Annas, carried away to Caiaphas —
what will he have to suffer here, alas, what will he
suffer there!?
And also look at Daniel, see,
how they taunt the prophet with their mockery!

CHOIR

„Let Daniel die! He who dares
to gossip and defame you, O King — you!
Let him be eradicated from Babylon!"
So speak the envious with drooling tongues,
the king has already decreed
is his punishment by death.

Alas, into the abyss he is thrown
he, Daniel, the prophet,
because of how he honored his God,
in chains he is to perish!
Now Jesus stands at his trial,
interrogated, questioned again.
As they pronounce his verdict blindly,
how is he to receive justice?
Consider the injustice of this world,
the tortures, sacrifices uncounted!
You who suffer so much misery,
hope for the Lord's justice!
Where the voice of truth is suffocated,
where the powerful suppresses it,
all you who stand there powerless, believe:
The Lord gives His love to justice!

THE MOCKERY OF JOB

BASS — SOLO
See here Job groaning in pain!
Alas, who does not shed a tear for him?
Laughing at him are his wife and friends
and mocking him to his face.

CHOIR
Alas, what strength —
see Job in pain!
But patiently he bears the plague.
Surrounded by mockery and ridicule,
he trusts in his God with hope.
Alas, what strength!
No sound of complaint leaves his mouth —
see Jesus how he endures it silently,
when he is insulted and beaten by brutality!
Oh give him compassion, since you can see,
how he stands before you humbled
in deepest disgrace,
the man of pain!
Alas, what strength!

INTERROGATIONS BEFORE ANNAS AND THE HIGH COUNCIL

Scene 1

ANNAS
Esdras, what is going on in the city?
ESDRAS
I do not know. From every alley people are running in
excitement towards the Mount of Olives.
ANNAS
In the middle of the night? Go, hurry to Kidron Gate
and see what is going on!

ESDRAS

As the high lord commands.

DATHAN

Caiaphas has gained a disciple of the Galilean who has revealed to him his nocturnal whereabouts.

ANNAS

So the waverer has finally acted!

DATHAN

He called an extraordinary meeting of the Council. I believe the Galilean is in our hands.

ANNAS

It would be a great fortune for the High Council if he were caught.

ESDRAS

Nathaniel is coming, I can see him hurrying down the street.

SELPHA

Do not spare him! Push him!

HORDE

Forward! Move, you false prophet!

NATHANAEL

High Lord, the Galilean has been caught.

ANNAS

What pleasant news! What blessed hour! I am so joyous, I must embrace you.

NATHANAEL

Judas kept his word.

ANNAS

The whole High Council is in your debt. Judas, your name will have an honorable place in our almanacs. —

JUDAS

What is going on here? You are leading him through the city like a criminal. Nathanael! Caiaphas ordered that he be brought to him in silence. — Where is the meeting with the high priest to take place? I have to be there.

NATHANAEL

Meeting? There is no meeting! A hearing will be held. The High Council will interrogate him this very night.

ANNAS

Judas, I am afraid judgment will be passed.

JUDAS

What? I did not deliver him to you for this purpose.

ANNAS

You delivered him, the rest is our affair.

JUDAS

Caiaphas gave me his word!

ANNAS

O Judas, it is better to trust in the Lord rather than to rely on people. The Galilean will be sentenced before the festivities even begin. — Thank you for your diligent and wise assistance!

NATHANAEL

You have done your duty, now go.

ANNAS

Wait. Nathanael, we are in his debt. Here take this! Thirty pieces of silver! An appropriate reward for your efforts.

JUDAS

No, let him go!

DATHAN

Judas, take the money and go.

JUDAS

Woe to me! What have I done?!

Scene 2

ANNAS

Has the day of our longing finally arrived! The false prophet is in our hands. — Jesus, son of the carpenter, look at me. I have heard people say: You want to change the traditions that were passed on to us by Moses. Well then, speak! Justify your teachings, which you have spread throughout the land and which you used to seduce the people!

JESUS

I preached publicly and for the whole world to see, I taught in synagogues and in the temple, and I never preached in secret. What are you asking me? You know what I said.

BALBUS

Is this how you answer the High Priest? *(Slaps Jesus in the face)*

JESUS

If I have spoken untruthfully, prove that it is not the truth! But if I have spoken truthfully, why do you slap me?

ANNAS

He still wants to defy us even now that his life is in our hands? For too long you have derided the remarks of our most illustrious teachers, called the pious customs we perform useless and said that we only do them for outward appearances. You denounced the virtue of the scribes as hypocrisy and disregarded the divine lectureship and priesthood.

JESUS

(to Annas) Follow my words, and you will know the truth, and the truth will set you free.

ANNAS

What is this? A new doctrine? — We are the children of Abraham and have never been anyone's servant. How can you say: You shall be freed?

JESUS

Whoever sins the way you have sinned, is a slave to sin. Only when you are free of sin, will you be truly free.

ANNAS

Are you trying to accuse me of a sin? You who were born in sin, are lecturing your High Priest? What are you making of yourself? Beelzebub, the highest demon controls your evil spirit!

JESUS

I do not follow an evil spirit, I follow God! Those who keep His word will not see death for eternity.

ANNAS

Abraham and the prophets died, but you say: If anyone follows his words, he will not see death. Are you greater than the prophets, greater than our father Abraham?

JESUS

You call Abraham your father? If you were children of Abraham, you would be doing God's works. — But you condemn them and seek to kill me! Someone who tells you the truth.

ANNAS

The truth is: The Lord did not send you. But you seduce the people to follow false teachings.

JESUS

Why will you not understand my words?

ANNAS

Because I do not like them.

Scene 3

DATHAN

The High Priest!

CAIAPHAS

Blessed be our fathers!

HIGH COUNCIL

Blessed be the God of our fathers!

CAIAPHAS

Is everyone gathered?

DATHAN

Everyone you invited.

NATHANAEL

Noble High Priest, here he is, as you commanded, the prisoner. Honor the head of the High Council! Honor the head of the High Council! *(pushes him to the ground)*

CAIAPHAS

I have long yearned for this moment. Where do you have his followers?

SELPHA

His followers scattered like frightened sheep. We did not think it was worth the effort to capture them.

CAIAPHAS

So let us bring this matter to an end.

NATHANAEL

>Jesus of Nazareth, you are accused —

Scene 4

(Joseph of Arimathea, Nicodemus and some other priests appear)

JOSEPH OF ARIMATHEA

>What is happening here? Caiaphas! You summon the council for a meeting in the middle of the night, but I and many of those who honor the Galilean are not invited.

CAIAPHAS

>What would your business be here?

NICODEMUS

>Caiaphas, you want to pass judgment on this man before he has been questioned, before an investigation, before a witness interrogation has taken place? Is that right and just? Is such a course of action worthy of the fathers of God's people?

ARCHELAUS

>Are you accusing the High Priest of an injustice? Do you know the rules of our law?

NICODEMUS

>I know the Law of Moses as you do, and I know that no sentence may be passed before a proper hearing of witnesses.

CAIAPHAS

>Nicodemus, everything has been prepared. Dathan has brought the necessary witnesses. — Bring them in!

JOSEPH OF ARIMATHEA

>What? Those are to testify against him? Untrustworthy hypocrites, who only tell you what you want to hear!?

NICODEMUS

>Caiaphas, look at what you are doing! You are to hold judgment in the name of the Lord, not in yours. With the Lord, our God there is no injustice, no prestige of person, no corruption.

ANNAS

You are blinded, carried away by the foolish words
of an itinerant preacher who has risen up against us,
the priests and scribes, and undermines all order in
Jerusalem.

SIMON OF BETHANY

Fathers, be guided by the fear of the Lord! God is with
you when you do justice. Keep and do justice!

CAIAPHAS

Simon, enough! Nathanael, go on now!

NATHANAEL

Jesus, son of Joseph from Nazareth, you are accused of
inciting the people to disobedience and condemning
the teaching of the fathers. You have dared to hold
blasphemous speeches and to commit acts of sacrilege.
— Honorable men stand here ready to prove the truth
of these charges with their testimony. Listen to them,
then you may defend yourself if you can!

ELIAB

I can testify before God that this man called the
priests and scribes hypocrites, savage wolves in sheep's
clothing and blind guides of the blind. He publicly
said that their deeds should not be followed.

GAD

I have seen him befriend sinners...tax collectors and
harlots. He went into their homes to eat with them.

ELIAB

I have seen that too.

GAD

I have heard from reliable people that he even talked
to pagans, even stayed with them for days.

NATHANAEL

What can you say in your defense against these
testimonies?

ARCHELAUS

He is silent. So he has no defense against them.

ELIAB

I saw him doing on the Sabbath what is forbidden by God's law with my own eyes.

JEHOSHAPHAT

Yes! Without hesitation he performed healings of the sick and crippled on the Sabbath.

EZEKIEL

He also convinced others to break the Sabbath.

GAD

Yes! He commanded one man to carry his bed home, another to wash in the pool of Siloah.

NATHANAEL

What can you say in your defense against these testimonies? Object to them if you can! —

ANNAS

He does not speak or gesture. So, the defiance he has shown against me has not yet passed.

ARCHELAUS

He does not dare to confess before the fathers of the people, before his judges, what he has boasted about in front of the people.

GAD

He said: I will tear down the temple built by men and in three days, I will build another one not made by humane hands.

EZEKIEL

What boastful, impudent speech! Forty — six years were spent to build this temple, and he wants to rebuild it in three days!

CAIAPHAS

I see: You think you can save yourself through silence.

NICODEMUS

Caiaphas, what are you accusing him of?

NATHANAEL

He has trampled on the law!

NICODEMUS

Did he not say that not an iota of it should be removed?

EZEKIEL

He has abolished the fasts and cleansings, desecrated
the Sabbath!

SIMON OF BETHANY

He healed the sick and cured the possessed!

ARCHELAUS

He is a glutton and a drunkard, a friend of tax
collectors and harlots!

CAIAPHAS

Silence!

JOSEPH OF ARIMATHEA

High Priest! Did no signs and wonders happen?

CAIAPHAS

Do not trust these signs, you cannot know whose
work they are.

JOSEPH OF ARIMATHEA

I confess, no one can work these signs unless God is
with him.

CAIAPHAS

Joseph!? If God is with him? You are getting lost in a
fantasy!

NATHANAEL

He is a false teacher — a deceiver who carries out his
deeds only through Beelzebub!

NICODEMUS

If his work is of Satan, it will be destroyed. But if it
stems from God, you cannot kill him. Caiaphas let go
of this man!

CAIAPHAS

Never!

NICODEMUS

He is inconvenient to you and gets in the way of your
actions.

ANNAS

He sees us as false coins! He keeps away from our
ways as if they were filth.

NICODEMUS

Yes, Annas! But he praises the righteous happily.

JOSEPH OF ARIMATHEA

You hold honor before people higher than honor

before God. Tend God's flock that was entrusted to you and care for it as it pleases God! Be no masters of those in your protection, but an example to your flock! Then, when the LORD appears, you will receive the crown of glory.

ANNAS

Should not reverence protect us from being made the object of his derision?

NICODEMUS

He is a living reproach to your sympathies.

JOSEPH OF ARIMATHEA

Embrace humility, for God resists the arrogant, but to the humble He gives His grace. Humbly bow to the strong hand of God, that He may exalt you in His time. Brothers and fathers, I exhort you to show him love.

ARCHELAUS

He dared to forgive sins, which only God himself may do.

ANNAS

He put himself above Abraham, claiming that he existed before Abraham. He claims to be greater than Solomon, the wisest of Israel's leaders.

NATHANAEL

Yes, he wants to be all of them at once: Elijah, David and a new Moses!

CAIAPHAS

I urge you, be silent!

JESUS

The stone that the builders rejected has become a cornerstone. Whoever falls on this stone will be shattered; on whom it falls, they will be crushed.

CAIAPHAS

What are you talking about?

JESUS

I tell you: The kingdom of God will be taken from you and given to those who bear the expected fruits.

EPHRAIM

Who could take it from us? You?

CAIAPHAS

Silence! Nazarene! Where does your entitlement come from? — Who appointed you as leader of Israel and judge over us? Speak!

ANNAS

He is a seducer and deceiver who, under the pretext of a mission, works towards revolution and turmoil, and tempts the people to fall into religious dedication. —

CAIAPHAS

Yes! — But far worse than any of these accusations is this: He made himself out to be the Son of God.

NICODEMUS

What are you accusing him of?

CAIAPHAS

He called God his Father.

NICODEMUS

God has called us sons.

JOSEPH OF ARIMATHEA

Do we all not preach: You are our Father!

CAIAPHAS

Joseph, do you not understand? He called God his Father, made himself the Son of God, thus making himself an equal to God. He will declare himself a king, then the Romans will come with their forces and destroy our city. Jesus of Nazareth, I, the high priest, adjure you by the living God! Tell us! Are you the Son of God, the Son of He who is worthy of praise? Are you the Messiah?

JESUS

I am he.

CAIAPHAS

He has blasphemed God! *(rips his robe)* What more do we need witnesses for? You have heard the blasphemy coming out of his mouth. Joseph, teacher of the law,

I demand you to answer: What does the holy law say about the blasphemer?

JOSEPH OF ARIMATHEA

„Tell the children of Israel: Whoever curses their God shall be held responsible. Whoever blasphemes the name of the Lord is to be put to death. The entire conjugation must stone them, whether they are foreigners or native-born."

CAIAPHAS

Thus it stands written, and it is your duty to pronounce judgment on the guilt and punishment of this person.

JOSEPH OF ARIMATHEA

I profess: According to his way, which you condemn, he serves the God of our fathers.

CAIAPHAS

Joseph! Have mercy on your land, on the temple, on our women and children, and do not put everything at risk because of one Galilean.

JOSEPH OF ARIMATHEA

He believes in everything that is written in the Law and the Prophets, and has the same hope in God that many of us here have.

CAIAPHAS

O you faithless and lost generation. Joseph, it is not me, not the High Council — he himself pronounces judgment on himself.

NATHANAEL

He is guilty of blasphemy!

ANNAS

Guilty!

JOSHUA

Guilty!

MANY

Guilty!

NICODEMUS

Brothers, fathers! Like you, I heard the teachings of the man from Nazareth and have seen his deeds!

What I know, I speak about. What I have seen, I testify to. But you do not accept my testimony.

JEHOSHAPHAT

Guilty!

DATHAN

Guilty!

PRIESTS

Guilty!

NATHANAEL

What are you still doing here, traitor of the High Council?

JOSEPH OF ARIMATHEA

No evidence could be found for anything that would make Jesus a criminal and no evidence for that will ever be found.

SIMON OF BETHANY

Your wounded vanity has twisted Jesus' speeches.

JOSEPH OF ARIMATHEA

You have all conspired against the will of God! Let him go! Do not be captivated by injustice!

CAIAPHAS

No one, Joseph, no one shall accuse us of any injustice. Listen, not only is he guilty of violating our law, but he also has violated Roman law on many counts. Not we, but the procurator Pontius Pilate will pass judgment on him. *(to Selpha)* Lead the prisoner into the courtyard and wait for our order!

JOSEPH OF ARIMATHEA

No! How can you, Caiaphas, hand over a son of Israel to the cruel Roman?

CAIAPHAS

You have no knowledge about these things!

JOSEPH OF ARIMATHEA

Have our fellow believers not suffered enough already! How many death sentences have been pronounced and most cruelly executed!

CAIAPHAS

Joseph, I do not have to justify my actions to you. —
Be silent now, you apostates!

SIMON OF BETHANY

Caiaphas! Pilate will kill him.

CAIAPHAS

Fathers! Listen to my word. I, the High Priest tell
you: It is better that one person perish than the whole
nation!

Scene 5

JUDAS

Caiaphas!

ARCHELAUS

Who is speaking?

JUDAS

Caiaphas, you misled me. You betrayed and deceived
me.

ARCHELAUS

How dare you push your way into our midst without
being called?

JUDAS

Is it true? Are you planning his death?

NATHANAEL

Get out of here! You will be called if you are needed.

JUDAS

I need to know. Have you sentenced him? — Woe to
you, Caiaphas! Woe to you! You condemn and murder
the innocent.

CAIAPHAS

Easy now, Judas!

JUDAS

No, no rest for me! No rest for you! The blood, the
blood of the innocent cries out to heaven.

CAIAPHAS

What is confusing your soul? Tell us!

JUDAS

You seek to hand over the one who is free from any
guilt to the Romans? You cannot do that. You will not

do that! I object. *(Laughter)* Yes, laugh! Mock me! I
have sinned. I betrayed the righteous one. Punish me,
Caiaphas, but spare Jesus!

EZEKIEL

Clear your mind, Judas! You received a respectable
reward.

JUDAS

I do not want it! Here you have your cursed, your
blood money back! *(Throws it down)* Now free the
innocent!

ARCHELAUS

Get a hold of yourself, you fool!

JUDAS

Caiaphas, you made me a traitor. I demand you
release the innocent one.

ANNAS

What, you shameful traitor soul, you want to dictate
rules to the High Council?

JUDAS

Me a traitor soul? Then tear me apart, you devil from
deepest hell!

ANNAS

Judas?

JUDAS

Crush me!

ANNAS

What a madman.

CAIAPHAS

Why did you let yourself do something that you had
not thought through beforehand? You betrayed your
friend — I am pursuing an enemy.

JUDAS

So shall my soul perish — my body burst — and you,
you shall rot with me in hell!

JEHOSHAPHAT

Caiaphas, do not tolerate this! Punish this audacious
man!

CAIAPHAS

Go! Go away!
(The temple guard leads Jesus out)

CAIN AND ABEL

TENOR — SOLO

„Come, O Death, my consoler! Come, O Death!
May my master and friend die.
Alas, now come and console me —
it would be an end to my misery!
Shall he perish through my fault?
Alas, how could I surrender my friend,
surrender him to death?
I have lost him, I have ruined him!
I cannot live with my guilt.
I have lost him, I have ruined him!
And so my life I take as well,
my life as well!"

CHOIR

He does not know how to close the gates of the abyss,
hot embers of despair are blazing high.
His conscience driving him into a rage,
tormented by all furies heat,
Judas rushes around ceaselessly
as he can no longer rest peacefully.

CONTRALTO — SOLO

Cain does also flee, but where to?
You cannot escape yourself,
inside of you reside the torments of hell.
And if you rush from place to place,
the scourge will swing on and on.
Wherever you are, you will be pursued!
Is there an end to your agony?
Where can there be salvation still?
Are you to bear your pain forever?

CHOIR

Behold, Judas falls into the dark!
Why does no brother catch him?

Lord, in you grace, let the outcasts,
the tormented and the restless,
the desperate and traitors,
the victims, and the perpetrators,
the fearful and the sinful
find peace and forgiveness with you!

JESUS IS MOCKED
PETER DENIES JESUS
JUDAS'S DESPAIR

Scene 1

JUDAS

Where can I go to hide my shame, to escape my agony? No place is dark enough. No sea is deep enough. Esdras!

ESDRAS

What do you want?

JUDAS

What are they planning on doing with him? I need to know! ... Do they want to kill him? No, no, they must not take it that far. It must not come to that! It would be terrible if they... and it would be my fault! If he had wanted to save himself, he would have revealed his power in the olive grove! But since he did not do it there —

RAM

— he will do it no more. *(laughter)*

GIDON

What happened?

PANTHER

They brought the Galilean to Annas. His defense went badly.

MELCHI

What? Badly? He got a good slap in the face because of it. *(laughter)*

SARAH

Men, come here. It is warmer here.

MELCHI

Hey, comrades, over here!

PANTHER

I like it here. I should have come sooner!

SARAH

Esdras, is the hearing over yet?

ESDRAS

No, it seems as if it will continue through the night. A heated dispute arose among the priests.

HAGAR

A dispute?

ESDRAS

Yes.

HAGAR

Do any of the elders believe in the Galilean?

ESDRAS

Joseph of Arimathea — also Nicodemus and some of the Pharisees spoke for him.

ARPHACHSHAD

That will not help him.

PETER

John, I am petrified of approaching this house.

JOHN

He is not here. You think they have taken him again?

PETER

How must Jesus have fared?

JUDITH

(to John) Hey, come here! Here you can warm yourself up.

PANTHER

A young cub for the old cat! *(laughter)*

JUDITH

Grant him a place at my side!

JOHN

There is another companion with me. May he join, too?

HAGAR

So there is one for me as well. Come!

JOHN

What happened? From afar, I saw people moving here through Kidron Gate, so I went after them to see what had happened.

ESDRAS

They brought a prisoner. He was brought before Caiaphas.

HAGAR

I know you, if I am not mistaken, you are one of the disciples of this Galilean.

PETER

Me? I am not the one you mean.

HAGAR

Look! Look, this one is a follower of the Galilean!

PETER

Woman, I do not know him, I do not even know what you are saying. (*Jesus is led out*)

ESDRAS

Selpha, how did it turn out?

SELPHA

Half the night they fought over him. We must guard him until dawn, then he will be taken to Pilate.

BALBUS

You can imagine what that means.

GIDON

What?

SELPHA

Pilate, the bloodhound, will sentence him to death.

GIDON

Oh dear! This must not happen! Come on, break free! Free yourself from your shackles!

HAGAR

(*to Peter*) You are lying. Of course you were with him.

SARAH

Yes, you were with the Nazarene!

PETER

No, I assure you — it was not me. I do not even know the man.

JUDITH

You are one of his disciples.

MELCHI

Yes, I saw you with him tonight in the olive grove.

GIDON

Arrest him!

PETER

Let go of me! *(is held)*

SELPHA

What is going on?

GIDON

This is one of the followers of the Galilean!

PETER

God be my witness: I do not know him! I do not know what has come over you. Why should I concern myself with that Jesus?

ARPHACHSHAD

Now you have given yourself away.

OBED

You know his name.

BALBUS

Yes, you are a follower of the Galilean.

RAM

Do you not recognize your rabbi? *(Peter breaks free and runs away)*

MELCHI

You will not escape us. *(to Jesus)* All your followers will be eradicated.

BALBUS

Comrades, look the dreamer is coming *(Jesus falls down)* You are pitiful — first you were a great man of miracles and now you are so weak and feeble.

OBED

Come, let your almighty thunder roar, let your lightnings come down!

MALCHUS

That they may feel your strength, throw them into the dust! *(Everybody drops down and laughs)*

SELPHA

Are you not a great prophet? Blindfold him! *(he is beaten)* Tell us, who beat you?

ARPHACHSHAD

Was it me?

MEMBER OF THE TEMPLE GUARD

Was it me?

LEVI

Was it me?

PANTHER

Or perhaps it was me?

OBED

Was it me?

BALBUS

Or was it me?

SELPHA

He is mute and deaf — what a great prophet! Come, Galilean, your followers want to proclaim you their king!

LEVI

Is this throne too modest, great king? Come your majesty, sit down!

BALBUS

Harder! You might want to fall down otherwise!

HAGAR

Greetings to you, our brand new king!

ALL

Greetings!

ARPHACHSHAD

Come! Let us help him back up on his throne!

GIDON

Arise, mighty king!

MELCHI

Receive our praise anew!

ALL

Praise be to you, exalted King! Praise to you!

LEVI

(Clears throat and spits in his face) Forgive me, I did not see you there. *(Slaps his face. Jesus falls down.)*

PANTHER

Oh dear, our king has fallen from his throne!

OBED

What are we supposed to do now? We no longer have a king!

BALBUS

Oh dear, who will save us now. Who will lead us?

SELPHA

We have no leader... abandoned by all..

DATHAN

Well, how is the new king doing?

SELPHA

He is good for nothing.

DATHAN

The High Priest sends me, it is time to bring him before Pilate!

SELPHA

Up now, Galilean! You have been king for long enough.

LEVI

Your reign is over now.

SELPHA

Take him and let us hurry to the procurator's palace! — Rejoice, Pilate will give you an exaltation! An elevation between heaven and earth.

BALBUS

There the ravens will sing around your ears. *(They lead Jesus away)*

Scene 2

PETER

Come here! Come here! Drive a lance into me, alas,
whip me, spit on me and defame me, break my bones.
Wretched man that I am! How low I have fallen! —
My friend and teacher, I have denied you — thrice I
denied you! Him for whom I had promised to sacrifice
myself!

MELCHI

Go, buy yourself a rope!

PETER

Curse my betrayal! Curse my shameful cowardice!

JOHN

(To Peter) He will not leave you. His glance when he
looked at you — believe me, he will forgive you.

PETER

To betray him! I cannot understand how I could forget
myself like this. — Jesus! If you still have mercy on
me, mercy for a treacherous man, send it to me! Hear
the voice of my repentant heart! The betrayal is over,
I cannot undo it. But never, never again will I let go of
you. All the love of my heart shall belong to you from
this moment on, binding me firmly and deeply to you!
And nothing, nothing shall ever be able to separate
me from you again!

Scene 3

JUDAS

No longer can I live. I betrayed him, the best of all
of us, delivered him into the hands of his enemies to
torture him, to execute him. Is there another person
as guilty as I am? Despicable traitor that I am! — May
the earth split open and devour me!
How good he was to me! How he comforted me
when grim resentment burdened my soul! How he
warned me when I was already planning my shameful
treachery! And this is how I repaid him.
Cursed Satan, you have made me blind and deaf! You

96

tricked me into committing this act, pulled me into
the abyss. No longer a disciple — an outcast — hated
everywhere, hated everywhere, loathed by everyone,
even my seducers call me traitor, and I wander around
with this blistering fire inside of me!

Everything turns away from me. Everything curses
me.

There is only one — one person left, whose face I
wish to see again, to whom I would hold onto. But he
is being led to death. Because of me! Because of me!
Woe to me! There is no more hope, no more salvation
for me.

He is dead and I am his murderer.

Ill — fated hour in which my mother gave birth to
me! Should I go on living this torturous life? Carrying
this agony inside of me? Fleeing from people like an
outcast? Being condemned by all the world? No, I
cannot stand it any longer! Not one more step wish
to take. This is where I want to end it, end this cursed
life. This is where the hapless fruit shall hang. Come,
you snake, get around my neck! Strangle this traitor.

IX. PRESENTATION
MOSES BEFORE PHARAOH

BASS — SOLO

    The death sentence, alas, it is spoken!
    Rejected is the Lord — banished the Holy One!
    O see him! Do you also want to cast out the one,
    sent to us from heaven?
    Repent!

CHOIR

    All you people! Look up to Jesus' bright light!
    Do not turn away from the source of salvation,
    that it may not close for you!
    So that the weight of darkness,
    bringing death and destruction,
    may not pour down upon you!

SOPRANO — SOLO

    Oh, Jesus taken away —
    surrendered to Pilate's judgement!
    And him who has come from down heaven,
    the Lord, he also does not know!
    Behold Moses! Behold, like Jesus, once cast out!
    The heart of the mighty one is closed to him as well!

BASS — SOLO

    „Remove yourself from my throne!
    Never will freedom be your reward!"
    so speaks Egypt's ruler coldly,
    „I have power over you!
    Never shall you return back home,
    to worship there another Lord
    and not me!
    You speak of Yahweh, a God,
    who sent you before my throne.
    Show me his face!
    His name is unknown to me!
    Never shall you leave, that shall ridicule me!
    Never will I follow your God,
    for I do not know your Yahweh!"

CHOIR
>
> And so the great prophet
> was rejected.
> Contempt was his only reward.
> And so they still do not recognize him,
> the one sent to us,
> so the Son of God was rejected!
> If your life is not open to God,
> then — as revealed in this world —
> hate for others will fill your heart!

JESUS BEFORE PILATE AND HEROD

Scene 1

SELPHA
>
> Push him!

PANTHER
>
> Do you expect us to carry you?

LEVI
>
> Go on! Your journey is a short one anyway!

MALCHUS
>
> You can rest at the gallows.

HORDE
>
> Away with you, you false prophet!

CAIAPHAS
>
> Now stay calm!

QUINTUS
>
> What do these people want?

ARCHELAUS
>
> The High Council has gathered here. I stand here
> requesting the emperor's exalted governor to receive
> the High Priest.

QUINTUS
>
> I will report it to the governor...

CAIAPHAS

Men of the High Council, if you are concerned with our standing, with peace for the whole country, remember this moment! It will be decided between us and that seducer.

Scene 2

(Pilate appears)

PILATE

What is all this yelling about? Leave!

CAIAPHAS

Procurator, I bow before you. I bow before the emperor, father of all Romans. I bow before...

PILATE

Yes! Enough! O All — mighty One, wrecking my dreams, go to the devil!

CAIAPHAS

How do you speak to the messenger of the Lord?

PILATE

Caiaphas, why are you bothering me? Is something happening in the city?

CAIAPHAS

I assure you, I have the city completely under control.

PILATE

And to tell me this, you bring your fellow priests into my courtyard and wake me up in the middle of the night.

CAIAPHAS

Sublime governor! I would never dare to do such a thing. I come before the procurator of the exalted emperor with a request to sentence Jesus of Nazareth, who rebelled against Roman law on many counts.

PILATE

Caiaphas! I told you that I never wanted to hear about this Jesus again. Priest, look at me! You dare to make me, the emperor's governor, look like a fool and disobey my orders. You dare to drag this street dog into my palace? — Why are you not facing me?

CLAUDIUS

Maybe he stole something. *(The soldiers laugh)*

ANNAS

He pretends to be the Messiah, the King of Israel.

PILATE

I know that. I know everything!

CAIAPHAS

Pilate, that is incitement of the people to rebel against the emperor.

PILATE

Rebellion — against the emperor!

CAIAPHAS

A call for rebellion....

PILATE

I admire his suddenly awakened fervor for the emperor's honor. —

ARCHELAUS

He has been interrogated by the Council and was found guilty. Therefore, it seems unnecessary, that the exalted governor should exhaust himself with further investigations.

EZEKIEL

So, sentence him!

PILATE

Where did you find those chickens cackling behind you?

CAIAPHAS

So, sentence him!

PILATE

What? You dare to see me, the emperor's representative, as your blind tool that carries out your rulings? If you have found him guilty, take him and sentence him yourself!

CAIAPHAS

Never, Procurator, never would we dare to do such a thing without your authorization. We are not allowed to pass the death sentence during your presence in the Holy City. The emperor has given you that authority.

PILATE

Now suddenly you are so well informed about
the emperor's instructions. — Caiaphas, I have
understood you. You are incompetent, you have lost
control over your crowd and that is why you want me
to get my hands dirty.

CAIAPHAS

Pilate, I beg you. It has to happen now! This very
night. Thousands of pilgrims will come to Jerusalem
for the Feast of the Passover. His followers are
scattered now, but we cannot allow them any time to
organize an uprising. You wanted him, now take him.

PILATE

Caiaphas, are you afraid of his followers!? People tell
me, even in your own ranks, even among your priests,
there are admirers of the Galilean.

CAIAPHAS

Pilate, is it not an insurrection when he forbids the
people to pay taxes to the emperor?

PILATE

(annoyed, to Jesus) Did you hear that? So, you have
instigated the people — Answer me! You called
yourself King of the Jews. What truth is there to it?
(Jesus is silent)

PILATE

You will not speak with me? In Jerusalem, people
whisper to each other that I am a cruel judge. And
they are absolutely right. Longinus, explain to him
that he has to talk to me!

LONGINUS

(Hits him) Do you understand? Speak!

PILATE

Jew! You are accused of making yourself king. Speak!
What truth is there to it?
(Jesus is silent)

PILATE

Do not be rebellious with me. You know that I have
the power to release you and power to crucify you.

JESUS

You have no power over me.

PILATE

What? I have no power?

(laughs)

Scene 3

(appearance of King Herod with entourage)

HEROD'S ENTOURAGE

The King of Galilee!

PILATE

King! — You are staying in Jerusalem for the feast?

HEROD

Like every year. And every year the same heat and every year the same...

HEROD'S ENTOURAGE

... dirt.

HEROD

(sees the many priests) Oh — the Lord's army!?

CAIAPHAS

Sublime King!

PRIESTS

Every blessing to you from the Almighty!

HEROD

Yes. Pilate, a pleasant message reached my ear. I hear you hold the famous man of miracles, Jesus of Nazareth, as your prisoner.

PILATE

Here he is.

HEROD

He? For a long time I wished to see him, the man, whose deeds are discussed in the whole country, whom the people follow in droves, as if won over by a magic touch!

PILATE

My King, if you take such great pleasure in him, take him, I give him to you!

HEROD

You are giving him to me? Oh Pilate! He shall be a proof of our friendship.

CAIAPHAS

Pilate, what are you doing?

PILATE

He is a Galilean and his subject.

CAIAPHAS

Why this new delay?

HEROD

Since I have met you so unexpectedly, I am very eager to test your miraculous powers. I have heard many, many things about you through the stories people tell and have long wished to see such the man who leaves whole countries marveling.

CAIAPHAS

King Herod, the High Council captured this seducer of the people and has brought him before the emperor's governor to be sentenced.

PILATE

Caiaphas, now let him enjoy this moment!

HEROD

I have heard that you see through people's secrets and do deeds that go beyond the limits of nature. Let us see a sample, a proof of your science and high power — and I will honor you with the people and believe in you!

ARCHELAUS

King, do not allow yourself to be misled, he is in league with Beelzebub!

HEROD

What do I care? Listen! If you are as enlightened as Joseph was when he stood before the king of Egypt, then interpret a dream for your king as he did! I was standing on the battlements of my palace at Herodium and watching the sun go down. Then, suddenly a figure appeared in front of me, stretched out its hand, pointed towards the evening sky and said: Look there, there is your bedchamber! No sooner had she said it than the figure dissolved into mist. It was like a fever dream; I tore out my hair, I cried, I prayed, I sang — I do not know how it was — I was startled and woke up. What does this mean?

(Jesus is silent)

PILATE

I do not think he is well-versed on the subject.

HEROD

What a pity. Then show us your famed miracle power! Use it to darken the sky at once!

ZEBULUN

Show yourself to be obedient! Please your king to earn his favor against the charges of your enemies!

HEROD

Or rise and walk before us without touching the ground.

EHUD

Come now, take your destiny into your hands and rise to the sky.

HEROD

Or turn that staff into a snake, as Moses once did!

ZEBULUN

Do you not want to —

HEROD

— or are you unable to? It should be easy for you, people talk about much more amazing miracles you worked. — He is not moving.

MANASSEH

If there is something to you, why does your wisdom fall silent here?

DELAIAH

Why does your power dissolve here like a bubble?

NAHSHON

It is easy to play illusions on the stupid people. It is something else to stand before the wise and powerful king.

HEROD

Yes, I can see that the tales that glorify him so much just are vain chatter people tell one another. He does not know or do anything! He is a foolish man whom the approval of the people has made a little crazy. His great deeds are lies and deception. Tales that only serve for seducing the people. He certainly did not fulfill my expectations. I promised myself the most pleasant delight, promised myself marvelous miracles and God knows what level of eloquence. John — you all know him — spoke with a wisdom and power that filled you with awe. But this one is as mute as a fish.

CAIAPHAS

King, do not trust this person! He only poses as a fool in order to obtain a more lenient sentence. — Pilate, time is short, this man must be sentenced before the festivities begin.

ANNAS

If we do not get him out of the way, even the king himself will be in danger, for he has declared himself a king.

HEROD

This one? *(to Pilate)* This one a king?

PILATE

He gathered masses by the thousands, and only a few days ago, he —

HEROD

— entered Jerusalem on a donkey, surrounded by women and children — so I heard.

PILATE

He is your subject. If you please, judge him!

HEROD

What? You are granting me the judgment over him? How can I be a judge in a foreign place? — No, Pilate, I will not be guilty of the death of a king. My sentence is: He is a simple-minded person and completely incapable of the crimes that you are accusing him of. If he did or said something that is against the law, he did so because of his naivety.

PILATE

King, be careful not to be mistaken!

HEROD

I am not mistaken. Just let him go! He is not worth your trouble.

Scene 4

PILATE

So once again I have to do everything myself.

ANNAS

He does not follow Rome and does not follow our law ... he called himself the Son of God....

RABINTH

We all heard the blasphemy coming from his mouth.

PILATE

Blasphemy?! Your religion bores me to death. Just because of such a speech, which is at most the fruit of a rapturous imagination, a Roman cannot sentence someone to death. Also, who is to know if this man is not the son of some other god?

CAIAPHAS

Pilate, I had your word that our law would be upheld.

PILATE

But I do not feel like wasting my time with your superstitious nonsense.

JESUS

You kings and governors of the world rule over your nations. You the powerful let yourselves be called benefactors. You take the sons of your people and push them into your wars. You take the best fields from the poor and give them to the rich. You rob the fathers of their daughters and make them slaves.

PILATE

Nazarene, my patience is running out. Well — are you the King of the Jews? —

JESUS

My kingdom is not of your world. If my kingdom were of your world, my soldiers would have fought for me so that I would not have fallen into the hands of my enemies. I was born and came into the world to bear witness to the truth. Everyone who is on the side of truth hears my voice.

PILATE

What is truth? *(beats him)* This is truth. Oh, had you not been born! — For the last time: Are you the king of the Jews?

JESUS

You have said it. I am he.

CAIAPHAS

Now he has told you himself.

QUINTUS

Pilate, he proclaimed himself king over Israel. This is high treason! He is a high traitor against Rome. So crucify him!

PILATE

(To Longinus) Let my soldiers take him. —

CAIAPHAS

What does this mean?

ARCHELAUS

What are you going to do?

PILATE

Control your curiosity and wait! *(To Jesus)* Now pray, Jesus of Nazareth, King of the Jews, pray to your God! And hope that he may help you in this hour! Whip him!

Scene 5

LONGINUS

    So come, your majesty, and allow me to accompany you! *(rips off his robe)*

DOMITIUS

    What an honor for us to walk alongside the King of the Jews!

LONGINUS

    Whip him! *(Jesus is scourged, collapses)*

BRUTUS

    Rise up!

GAIUS

    Strike him!

LONGINUS

    Do not spare your strength!

TITUS

    Harder! Even if he should collapse on the way! *(Jesus collapses)*

PILATE

    Do not cripple him! I still need him. Continue! *(Jesus collapses)* Behold this man. Look at him, you priests, and be warned! Serve the emperor with awe and kiss his feet with trembling, lest he be angry and you perish!

CAIAPHAS

    Pilate, do you know what you are saying?

PILATE

    I know what I am saying. Continue!

PEDIUS

    I cannot go on, my arms are getting tired.

MILO

    What? Tired? With every blow, my strength is growing.

    (beating continues, Jesus collapses)

CLAUDIA

    Stop it! Stop it! You are beating him to death!

BRUTUS

    How can he die? He is God after all! *(All laugh)*

CLAUDIA

Pilate, I beg you, release him! I suffered fear and terror in a dream tonight because of him.

PILATE

I am also haunted by dreams, Claudia. It is that damn heat in this land that keeps us from sleeping.

CLAUDIA

Pilate, do not mock me! I see a righteous man, the only righteous man, surrounded by injustice and violence.

PILATE

Go, woman! *(to the soldiers)* Continue!

GAIUS

Get up! *(beating continues, Jesus collapses)*

LONGINUS

He has had enough now! You pitiful king of the Jews!

PILATE

But what kind of king is he? Without a scepter in his hand? Without a crown on his head?

BRUTUS

We can help with that — he shall be royally vested.

PEDIUS

Be patient for a while, I will be right back!

MILO

You must become a true king.

HEROD

Pilate, I want to give him a royal cloak and formally proclaim him king of all fools!

BRUTUS

Behold this magnificent royal cloak! This is certainly a most lovely ornament for a Jewish king.

MILO

You did not expect such an honor, is that true?

BRUTUS

Come, let us put the purple cloak on you!

PEDIUS

And here a wonderfully sculpted crown! — Let me
look at you!

TITUS

But in order for it to not fall off his head, you have to
put it on him firmly. *(presses the crown on his head)*

MILO

And here — the scepter! Now you have all you need.
What a king!

PEDIUS

Hail to you, mightiest king of the Jews!

ALL

(kneel down before him) Hail to you, mightiest king of
the Jews!

PILATE

Caiaphas, you told me about the incidents in the
temple district. Hundreds accompanied this Jesus to
the atrium, calling him Son of David, throwing clothes
at his feet and scattering palms. The people love this
dreamer. I realize that now. I want to give them a little
treat. Caiaphas! They want a king, and I will give
them a king.

LONGINUS

(laughs loudly) They will feel lucky to get such a
handsome king.

PILATE

With this king all the nations will have nothing but
scorn and derision for you. Now go no and do not
forget your King!

CAIAPHAS

Pilate, you are making us look ridiculous. The people
of Jerusalem know that you will persecute them with
great hatred and cause them many more torments, but
you will never ruin them. God will protect them. He
will hear our prayers, and also the mighty emperor
will hear us and protect us from Pilate the corrupter.
Do you hear me, Pilate?!

PILATE

I hear you — I have heard your voice! The croaking voice of a man who not so long ago was put on the chair of the High Priest by none other than myself! Caiaphas, here in Jerusalem only the voice of the procurator is valid. Be wary of me! I repeat, be wary of me!

CAIAPHAS

We do not want this king.

(Pilate departs)

CAIAPHAS

He ridicules and mocks us. Go to every street and alley of our Holy City and call our followers to come here! Seek to win over the fickle by the power of your words! But intimidate the followers of the Galilean so that no one dares to show his face here!

EZEKIEL

We will be back soon.

JEHOSHAPHAT

From every alley of Jerusalem, let us bring the agitated people before the judgment hall.

NATHANAEL

Each with a fervent flock!

CAIAPHAS

Pilate hear the many — voiced call: The Galilean to the cross!

ALL

The Galilean to the cross! (Caiaphas and the priests depart)

TENOR — SOLO

O Jesus, King!
In mockery
you were crowned!
Alas, with what crown
and what a scepter in your hand!
We see you dressed in purple,
the mocker's lust feasts on your sight.
Why do you endure the pain and ridicule?
What, O Lord, brings you into this misery?

CHOIR

Behold, the man!

TENOR — SOLO

Jesus! King! Crowned in mockery!

CHOIR

No trace of divinity left on him,
just a game for the crud executioners:
Behold, the man!

BASS — SOLO

Ecce, ecce homo!

TENOR — SOLO

Behold, the man!
Pilate said full of contempt,
when he saw the Lord, bruised and scourged,
standing there, tied with a rope.
When Joseph once in wisdom
interpreted the dream of the seven plagues
an ecstatic song of praise was sung for him,
to give thanks to the Savior.

JOSEPH INTERPRETS THE PHARAOH'S DREAM

CHOIR
> Loud shall it echo through Egypt:
> Long live Joseph, high and mighty!
> And a thousand times it shall echo:
> The people's savior, friend he is!
> And the joyful sound of all the voices
> may resound for you in praise!

SOPRANO — SOLO
> You are Egypt's salvation and joy!
> You will free the land from misery and suffering!
> You, Joseph, Egypt praises today
> as savior — full of gratitude.

CHOIR
> Loud shall it echo through Egypt:
> Long live Joseph, high and mighty!
> And a thousand times it shall echo:
> The people's savior, friend he is!
> And the joyful sound of all the voices
> may resound for you in praise!

SENTENCING OF JESUS BY PILATE

Scene 1

LONGINUS
> Caiaphas and the High Council are herding together
> their followers from every house and alley. — They
> demand the release of Barabbas.

PILATE
> Barabbas!... Gods, what scum they are! I hate this city.

NICODEMUS

John, why were you not more vigilant!

JOHN

How has Jesus fared since I last saw him in the court of Caiaphas?

NICODEMUS

I do not know! Where did Peter go?

JOHN

I last saw him in the atrium of the High Priest. We followed Jesus there. Then we lost him in the crowd.

LAZARUS

Nicodemus, from every alley throngs of agitated people are coming together.

JOHN

What is happening in the city?

LAZARUS

I do not know!

NICODEMUS

The priests have left the palace. Early in the morning they took Jesus to the governor, but no one knows what is happening there.

JOHN

He himself told us: The Son of Man will be handed over to the High Priest and scribes, they will hand him over to the Romans. But they will mock him, whip him and kill him.

NICODEMUS

May God direct the mind of the governor to justice, that he may protect the innocent!

JOHN

A human life is not worth much to Pilate.

NICODEMUS

He urged us to be steadfast — now we must trust his word!

LAZARUS

The shouting is getting closer! I do not dare to go out on the street anymore!

SIMON OF BETHANY

Nicodemus!

NICODEMUS

Simon! What is that noise?

SIMON OF BETHANY

No one knows what is happening in the procurator's palace. We had little time to alert our friends.

JOSEPH OF ARIMATHEA

Show courage! Endure without fear! Whatever happens, the righteous cause will protect us. Shout it out on every market: Jesus is without guilt!

JOHN

Jesus is without guilt!

SOME

Jesus is without guilt!

Scene 2

NATHANAEL

I urge you: Save Jerusalem, Save our holy city!

SOME

You are our fathers! For you, we rise up!

EZEKIEL

Cast off the yoke of the seducer!

SOME

We no longer wish to have anything to do with him! We follow you.

ARCHELAUS

Follow the High Council! They will save you!

OTHERS

You are our teachers.... We want to be free from the false prophet, the Nazarene!

NICODEMUS

Brothers, do not listen to them! Which of the prophets did they not persecute?

NATHANAEL

Look there — Joseph with his followers! What a pitiful pile! *(Laughter)* Be faithful to your priests and teachers! Away with anyone who rises up against them!

SERVANTS OF CAIAPHAS

Leave!

NICODEMUS

You call yourselves teachers — you are full of injustice, malice and envy. Brothers! Do not listen to them! They slander, defame, are arrogant, haughty, ostentatious, without love and mercy.

JOSEPH OF ARIMATHEA

We are witnesses to all that Jesus from Galilee did until now here in Jerusalem, how he went around the land doing good and healing all those who were in the power of evil.

ARCHELAUS

He distorted the law.

NATHANAEL

He condemned Moses and the prophets!

EZEKIEL

He blasphemed God! We will not rest until he is sentenced.

NATHANAEL

The High Priest!

ANNAS

Come, children! Come to us, throw yourselves into the arms of the High Council! We will save you.

CAIAPHAS

Your fathers' God will welcome you back.

ARCHELAUS

Long live the High Council!

SOME

Long live our teachers and priests!

JOSEPH OF ARIMATHEA

Caiaphas! Why has your heart decided to do this?

CAIAPHAS

O ignorant ones, I pity you that you do not understand! As long as the Nazarene lives, there will be no peace in Israel! He considers himself above the law and the prophets! He believes he is beloved by God, that we should listen to his voice! He speaks in the temple as if he were the Messiah, the anointed servant of God.

ANNAS

This person does not stop holding speeches against the temple and against our law.

JOSEPH OF ARIMATHEA

He never presumed to annul even one iota of the law or the prophets.

NATHANAEL

Did we not forbid him to teach in the temple. But he filled Jerusalem with his teachings.

EZEKIEL

He held blasphemous speeches against Moses and the priests!

CAIAPHAS

Silence! Terrible is the misguiding power of the Galilean. It must be broken. If we allow him to go on, everybody will believe in him, rebellion will arise and then the Romans will come and take our temple and our people. I am the one who will keep the Lord's flock together. Why will you not understand! It is better that one person has to die before the whole country falls into ruin.

ARCHELAUS

Death to the false prophet!

PEOPLE

He must die!

JOSEPH OF ARIMATHEA

Him you want to kill? Go away from here!

AMAN

The blasphemer has to die!

SOME

He must die! He must die! He must die! He must die!

NICODEMUS

I curse that word. I will have no part in this shameful judgment.

NATHANAEL

Follow the High Priest and do not be misled by those!

CAIAPHAS

We will see who will prevail, you who follow of pagans, tax collectors and harlots, or we with adherence to those who abide by the law.

SOME

You we follow.... Long live the High Council! ... Long live the High Council!

CAIAPHAS

O rejoice that you have escaped the nameless perdition that this Galilean and his followers wanted to bring upon you!

ANNAS

Only the restless aspirations of your fathers will save you from the abyss.

CAIAPHAS

Listen to me: The governor has mocked us all. Just to shame us, he wants to release this rebel. Let us insist on the release of Barabbas!

ANNAS

Curse those who do not vote for his death!

EZEKIEL

We demand his death.

SOME

His death!

JOSEPH OF ARIMATHEA

Jesus is without guilt!

SOME

Release him... he is without guilt.

ANNAS

Outcast from our commune be he! No share shall he have in the heritage of our fathers!

JOSEPH OF ARIMATHEA

Jesus, Jesus is without guilt!

OTHERS

Jesus is without guilt!

NATHANAEL

Release Barabbas!

SOME

Release Barabbas!

OTHERS
> Jesus is without guilt!

ARCHELAUS
> Let the Nazarene perish!

SOME
> He must die! Down with the traitor!

Scene 3

QUINTUS
> What is going on here?

CAIAPHAS
> Be steadfast! Now demand judgment vehemently!

EZEKIEL
> Let the Nazarene perish!

SOME
> Let the Nazarene perish!

POMPONIUS
> Riot! Outrage!

EZEKIEL ARCHELAUS NATHANAEL JEHOSHAPHAT
> Let the Nazarene die!

SOME
> Die! Die! Die! Die!

OTHERS
> Jesus is without guilt! Release him.

SOME
> Die! Die!

ARCHELAUS
> Pilate must sentence him to die!

SOME
> The death sentence! The death sentence!

POMPONIUS
> Silence! Silence!

NATHANAEL
> No! We will not rest until Pilate releases Barabbas.

POMPONIUS
> Pilate will appear in a moment.
> *(Pilate appears)*

EZEKIEL
Release Barabbas!

NICODEMUS
Jesus is without guilt!

SOME
Barabbas!

OTHERS
Jesus is without guilt! Release him.

PILATE
Caiaphas, you bewilder me.

CAIAPHAS
Governor, hear the voice of the people of Jerusalem!
Look! They agree with our claims, they demand the
death of the Nazarene!

SOME
We demand his death!

PILATE
This is not the people of Jerusalem, it is an incited
mob.

NICODEMUS
Pilate, release Jesus, he is without guilt.

OTHERS
Release him!

EZEKIEL
On the cross he shall atone for his sacrileges!

PTOLEMY
On the cross!

SOME
Crucify him!

PILATE
Silence! People of Jerusalem! Listen! It is customary
to release a prisoner to you during the feast. *(Jesus is
brought)* Behold this man! Behold — your king! I give
him to you. Take your king and leave!

JEHOSHAPHAT
Take this one! Give us Barabbas!

PRIESTS
Release Barabbas!

CAIAPHAS

You want to release Jesus of Nazareth only so that he can instigate the people, defame our faith and bring the Roman sword upon our people. I, the High Priest of Judea, will protect the faith and my people throughout my entire life. Do you hear, Pilate?

PRIESTS

Crucify him!

NATHANAEL

Release Barabbas!

SOME

Release Barabbas!

PILATE

Silence! You demand the release of the rebel Barabbas? The release of a murderer who spread fear and horror throughout the city, who nefariously stabbed people in broad daylight?! Who dared to enter Jerusalem with his followers and proclaimed himself to be the ruler of the people. You seem to have forgotten that. I ask you Caiaphas: knowing this, do you want to reconsider?

CAIAPHAS

You will release the one the people demand.

JOSEPH OF ARIMATHEA

Release Jesus! He is without guilt!

NATHANAEL

Let Barabbas live!

SOME

Let Barabbas live!

NATHANAEL

Sentence the Nazarene to death!

EZEKIEL

To death the Nazarene!

SOME

Crucify him! ... Crucify him!

OTHERS

Release him! ...Release him! He is without guilt!

PILATE

What? You want me to crucify your king?

ANNAS

We have no king but the emperor alone.

NATHANAEL

Let Barabbas live!

SOME

Let Barabbas live! To death!

OTHERS

Jesus! Release Jesus!

PRIESTS

Release Barabbas!

SOME

Barabbas!

OTHERS

Free Jesus!

PILATE

People of Jerusalem! — I heard your pleas, crowned him for you, and now you do not want your king?

ANNAS

Israel does not want a king who can be caught and bound and mocked.

ARCHELAUS

Let him die, the false Messiah, the deceiver!

SOME

He must die! Crucify him!

PILATE

I do not understand you. A few days ago you accompanied this man, cheering and applauding, through the alleys of Jerusalem. You spread your garments before him, praising God for all the miracles he had done and shouting with loud voices: Blessed be the one who has come, the King, in the name of the Lord. Is it possible that you are calling for his death and demise today?

CAIAPHAS

They finally realized that they have been deceived by a madman who presumes to call himself Messiah, King of Israel.

NATHANAEL

Now their eyes have been opened as they see how he

cannot help himself, he who promised them freedom
and salvation.

CAIAPHAS

Pilate! Allow me to ask a question! Why are you not
sentencing this Galilean, since not long ago you had
your soldiers murder hundreds of people who were
only shouting rebellious cries, without judgment or
sentencing?

PILATE

I appointed you as priest, as warden over your people,
over all the lunatics who pretend to be prophets, to
put them in the stocks with an iron collar around their
necks, so I ask you, why are you not punishing him?

CAIAPHAS

Why should I kill a son of my people? Was it not you
who said: „If there is conflict in the land and rebellion
against Rome, I will come with military forces and
bring destruction to you, your land and your people."
— Well! You threatened to ravage the land if this one
seduces the people. You wish for his death. So crucify
him. Crucify him and there will be peace in this...

PILATE

... goddamn land!

CAIAPHAS

Pilate — if you let this one go, you are no friend of the
emperor.

PILATE

Say that again! Say that again, Caiaphas!

CAIAPHAS

If you let this one go, you are no friend of the
emperor.

PILATE

Careful now, High Priest! Watch your tongue!

CAIAPHAS

I do not fear you. All the blood you shed, — all the
violence and all the injustice you practice, cries out
to heaven, echoes with power, roars before your deaf
ears. Jesus of Nazareth proclaimed himself a king. And
whoever proclaims himself a king is a rebel against the
emperor.

NATHANAEL

And this rebel is supposed to leave without punishment and continue to sow the seeds of sedition?

ARCHELAUS

It is the duty of the governor to get him out of the way.

ANNAS

If unrest and indignation arise because of this man, we will know who is to blame, and the emperor will know as well. People in Rome will be astonished when they hear that the emperor's governor protected a high traitor.

NATHANAEL

You will have him executed or there will be no peace in the land.

PEOPLE

He has to die! ... To the cross with him! ... Release him! ... He is without guilt! ... Crucify him! ... Crucify him! ...Release Barabbas!... Free Jesus! ... Barabbas! ... Jesus! Release Jesus! ... Let Barabbas live!

JOSEPH OF ARIMATHEA

Brothers! In the name of our God, let there be no divisions among you, embrace one another with one mind and in one opinion. Can you not see, the Roman is sowing discord between us. Discord and fraternal war.

JEHOSHAPHAT

We will not move from here until the verdict is given.

PEOPLE

He has to die! ... To the cross with him! ... Release him! ... He is without guilt! ... Crucify him! ... Crucify him! ... Release Barabbas! ... Free Jesus! ... Barabbas! .... Jesus! ... Release Jesus! ... Let Barabbas live!

CAIAPHAS

Stop! I have fulfilled my duty as a subject of the emperor and handed this rebel over. Look at him! His malicious grin! In his heart he has already decided to kill Jesus.

PILATE

The Jew has seen through me. The death sentence for Jesus has already been written. King today, dead tomorrow! Water! — Barabbas be set free at your demand. Take him away — out to the city gate, that he may never tread this ground again! But know this: This very day a message will leave for Rome that you, Caiaphas, are saving rebels against Rome from the death penalty. ... High Priest, from now on you will have no rest. Whatever happens now and from now on, I wash my hands of it!

FAUSTUS

You want to leave!? Push them away, the scum of humanity!

LONGINUS

This will be worthy company for your king on his final journey!

PILATE

(To the two murderers) The earth shall be cleansed from you and your crimes today. You shall die on the cross. — May the death sentence be pronounced now!

QUINTUS

I, Pontius Pilate, governor of Emperor Claudius Tiberius in Judea, hereby pronounce the death sentence on Jesus of Nazareth, who is accused of inciting the people to turmoil, forbidding them to pay taxes to the emperor, and proclaiming himself to king of the Jews. He is to be nailed to the cross outside the walls of the city between two criminals who are equally condemned to death for several acts of murder, and brought from life to death. Given at Jerusalem on the eve of the Passover, in the eighteenth year of the reign of Emperor Tiberius.

(While Quintus reads, the crosses are brought)

PILATE

So take him and crucify him!

LONGINUS

Let our procession go through the midst of Jerusalem, so that everyone may see it!

POMPONIUS
Where are his followers to shout Hosanna?

FLAVIUS
His followers will quickly scatter, this Jesus will soon be forgotten.

AGRIPPA
Away with him to Golgotha, the place of the skull!

JOSEPH OF ARIMATHEA
John, heaven and earth will pass away; but his words will never pass away.

SACRIFICE OF ISAAC ON MOUNT MORIAH

CHOIR

> Silently you accept the Roman's sentence,
> that imposes the burden of the cross upon you!
> Doomed to die you waver to the last place of torture,
> bent, stripped of all dignity!

> Worship and give thanks to him,
> who drank the cup of suffering,
> who now goes to the death by the cross
> and reconciles the world to God!

CONTRALTO — SOLO

> As the sacrificial wood once taken
> by Isaac himself to Moria,
> now wavers — carrying the cross as burden —
> Jesus goes forth to Golgotha!
> All the trust he has in God
> helps him in this fear and torment
> despite the pain and deathly dread —
> to be sure of the path he treads.

CHOIR

> Worship and give thanks to him!
> who drank the cup of suffering,
> who lets himself be led like a lamb,
> to death on the cross.

SALVATION BY LOOKING UP TO THE BRONZE SERPENT

BASS — SOLO

> Nailed to the cross now
> he is raised, the Son of Man.

See, with Moses' serpent here
the model that the cross does follow:
From the poisonous bite of the serpent
came liberation to the people,
And so, from the cross will flow
salvation and bliss upon us!

CHOIR

Worship him and give thanks!
He who drank the cup of suffering,
walks the way of the sorrows crowned with thorns,
until he reconciles the world to God!

THE WAY OF THE SORROWS AND THE CRUCIFIXION

Scene 1

SIMON OF CYRENE

Children, come! We must go to the city! The Sabbath is about to dawn. We have little time to buy what we need to get home in due time.

SON OF SIMON

We will be right there!

LAZARUS

The streets are empty. Everything around us seems deserted.

MARY

Now I stand within your gates, Jerusalem. Peace be within your walls! By my son's will, I wish you peace, by the will of the temple of the Lord, our God, I invoke happiness for you. With every moment my grief over the fate of my son increases. Where are we going that I can see him? I need to see him — but where can I find him?

LAZARUS

The best would be, to go to Nicodemus, there we will find out what happened to Jesus.

(John comes)

JOHN

Cry, you gates! Wail, you walls! Be consumed by sorrow, Israel! Cry out loud to the Lord, daughter of Zion! Let your tears flow like a river day and night! Lord! Look and see: To whom have you done such things?

MAGDALENE

John what happened?

MARY

How did my son fare?

JOHN

Mary, the hour has come that he foretold.

MAGDALENE

Like a cloud, my hope vanishes. My soul is dissolving inside of me. I hoped for good, but evil comes. I waited for light, but darkness comes.

JOHN

All who see him mock him, open their mouths and yell. He is no longer a human. Beaten, whipped, ridiculed by the people, condemned by the people!

MARY

Thoughts are revealed! Now everything comes to light! O Simeon, now the prophecy you once told me will come true: He is destined to cause the falling and rising of many in Israel, and to be a sign that will be spoken against. But you will have to suffer many pains because of this child. *(Noise comes from the alley)* What mortal terror penetrates my heart suddenly.

JOSEPH OF ARIMATHEA

Mary, leave this place — you will not bear the sight of it!

MARY

Do not urge me to leave him or to turn back! Where he goes, I will also go.

SIMON OF BETHANY

You could be harmed yourself if they recognize you as his mother!

MARY

I want to suffer with him. I want to share his shame with him.

SIMON OF BETHANY

If only your strength does not fail!

Scene 2

VOICES FROM FAR AWAY

Continue! On with him!

SON OF SIMON

What is that noise?

SON OF SIMON

What is happening in the city? Come!

AGRIPPA

Is the weight already getting too heavy?

SOME

Crucify him! He must die!

SON OF SIMON

Father, the yelling!

SON OF SIMON

It seems that someone is being led to Golgotha to be executed.

SIMON OF CYRENE

Come away from here.

LONGINUS

Do not let him rest! Move! Push him with your strikes! Your wavering will not save you. You must go out to Golgotha.

JOSEPH OF ARIMATHEA

The crowd is squeezing through this gate. Come! Away from here!

NERO

You can rest on the cross.

LONGINUS

Push him with force so we finally reach Golgotha!

FAUSTUS

Stop! He is collapsing.

MARY

That is him. It is my son. My Jesus.

SOME

On with him!

LONGINUS

Get rid of the womenfolk! It is time to move forward.

CATILINE

What good are your tears? Back off!

NERO

Move, lazy King of the Jews!

SILVIUS

He might not make it all the way.

LONGINUS

Here, recover some strength! You do not want to drink? Then push him!

SILVIUS

Rise up!

VERONICA

What are you doing to him?

AGRIPPA

Whoever lies like that on the ground, will not get up again.

FAUSTUS

Gather your strength!

VERONICA

What ridiculous commands!

FAUSTUS

Shut your damned mouth!

SILVIUS

He is too weak.

LONGINUS

Someone must help him! — You! Come here!

SIMON OF CYRENE

Me?

LONGINUS

Yes you, you have broad shoulders that can carry some weight!

SIMON OF CYRENE

No, I have to —

NERO

Yes, you must!

SIMON OF CYRENE

Leave me alone!

FAUSTUS

Do not refuse! Or my arm will make you regret it.

LONGINUS

Hit him if he does not comply!

SIMON OF CYRENE

I am innocent. I have done nothing wrong.

LONGINUS

Silence!

SIMON OF CYRENE

Jesus...

CATILINE

Give us your shoulders!

AGRIPPA

Behold, King of the Jews, even the cross is taken from you!

FAUSTUS

So off you go, to the hill of death!

LONGINUS

Do not spare him! What does the woman want?

JOHN

Leave her — it is his mother!

MARY

Oh, seeing you, led to your death, like a criminal between criminals. — A sword pierces my soul.

LONGINUS

Continue!

SIMON OF BETHANY

Mary, come! Whatever happens, it is God's providence.

JOHN

You think he is was beaten up by God, struck and bent by Him? No! He was beaten because of our crimes, crushed because of our sins. The Lord charges him with the guilt of us all. He is abused and pressed down, but he does not open his mouth. Like a lamb led to slaughter, he does not open his mouth.

MARY

Lord, why have you wrapped yourself in clouds? No prayer can pierce them! You have made him filth and waste in amidst the nations. Tears, pour forth without ceasing! Do not stop until the Lord looks down from heaven and sees! Do not close your ear to my grieving, my crying!

VERONICA

Your face is covered with blood and sweat! Rabbi, this is how you are rewarded?

JESUS

Daughters of Jerusalem, do not weep over me; weep for yourselves and your children!

VERONICA

How will we and our children fare?

JESUS

There will come a time when people will say: Blessed are the barren, and the wombs that never bore children, and the breasts that never nursed. They will shout to the mountains: Fall on us! And to the hills: Cover us up!

CHOIR

Eli, eli lama asabtahni
My God, my God, why have you forsaken me,
rahohk mi shuwaty divrey sha'agati!
you are far from my cry, my lament!
Elohay ekrah yomam weloh ta'aneh
My God, I call by day and you do not answer,
welayellah weloh dumiahli!
and by night, and yet I find no peace.

Yavesh kaheres kohiy
My soul is as dry as a shard of clay,
ulshoniy mudbag malgohay
my tongue sticks to my gums,
weleá par mawet tischpeteny.
you set me in the dust of death!
Kammayim nishpachti
I have been poured out like water,
wehitparduh kol azmotay
all my limbs have dissolved.
haya libbi kaddonag,
My heart is like wax,
names betoch mehay
it melts away inside of me

Scene 3

NERO

The cross stands firm.

CATILINE

Come brothers! Let us share the spoils.

ANNAS

What is the purpose of the inscription „Jesus the Nazarene, King of the Jews"?

ARCHELAUS

This is mockery, insult to the council and the people!

AMAN

We cannot leave this inscription.

NATHANAEL

This title must go!

CAIAPHAS

We are not allowed to remove it ourselves. — I demand the amendment of this inscription. He is not our king! Write down that he claimed: „I am the King of the Jews."!

LONGINUS

This inscription was attached to the cross by order of the governor.

NATHANAEL

Tear it down!

PRIESTS

Tear it down!

LONGINUS

What was written will remain on the cross!

NATHANAEL

Unacceptable!

ARCHELAUS

If you are the Messiah, come down from the cross so that we may see it and believe in you!

EZEKIEL

You who wanted to tear down the temple of God and rebuild it in three days, now help yourself!

ANNAS

You trusted in God. May He save you now, if He loves you!

AGRIPPA

Now, come down and show your power, exalted King of the Jews!

NERO

Do you not hear?

CATILINE

Gone is all his strength. Soon the vultures will eat him.

JESUS

Father, forgive them, for they know not what they do!

GESTAS

If you are the Anointed One, the Messiah, save yourself now — and us with you!

DISMAS

Even you do not fear God, since you are condemned to the same punishment? It serves us right: We receive the just recompense for our crimes. But he has done nothing wrong. — Lord, remember me when you come into your kingdom!

JESUS

This very day you will be at my side in paradise.

CAIAPHAS

Do you hear that! He still acts as if he has the command over the gates of paradise!

ARCHELAUS

Has he still not lost his arrogance as he hangs helplessly on the cross?

MARY

My eyes look yearningly at you! What should I say? And what should I tell you since you did it yourself? Lord, my God! I am suffering misery! Help me!

JESUS

Mother, behold your son! — John, behold your mother!

JOHN

I will honor her as my mother. You — my mother! And I — your son!

JESUS

I am thirsty.

LONGINUS

He suffers thirst and calls for a drink.

CATILINE

Let him have it.

FAUSTUS

Here! Drink!

JESUS

Eloi! Eloi! Lama Sabachtani!

RABINTH

Listen, he is calling Elijah!

EZEKIEL

Let us see if Elijah comes to take him down from the cross of disgrace.

CAIAPHAS

He does not call for Elijah. He cries out for God who has abandoned him.

JESUS

It is done. — Father, into your hands I commit my spirit. *(Dies)*

CHOIR

Weattah, adonai, al tirhak,
But you, Lord, do not stay away,
ki zarah kerowah.
when distress approaches!

LONGINUS

Such patience in the most violent pain! The calmness!
The cry to heaven in the throes of death! This was a
righteous man!

MAGDALENE

Rabbuni! What held me has been killed, my soul, lives
for you.

SIMON OF CYRENE

What is this? The earth is shaking — the sun eclipses!

PEOPLE

Woe to us!

LONGINUS

The deity speaks through these terrors of nature —
truly, this man was God's Son!

RABINTH

Come — I will no longer stay in this place of horror!

ERES

May God have mercy on us!

RABINTH

Lord Almighty, we have sinned! Spare us!

ESDRAS

High Priest! Terrible things have happened in the
sanctuary!

CAIAPHAS

But not the temple!

ESDRAS

The curtain of the sanctuary is torn in two!

CAIAPHAS

Go and see what has taken place! I will not leave this
place until I see the body of that man thrown down
into the pit.

NICODEMUS

Caiaphas, he is dead! Will you never stop chasing him?

QUINTUS

Longinus, the governor has sent me to ask you if Jesus of Nazareth is really dead already, as this man here has reported to him.

LONGINUS

It is true. See for yourself —

QUINTUS

By order of the procurator, the legs of the crucified are to be broken, then their bodies removed! Everything shall be done, before the Sabbath dawns.

LONGINUS

It will happen at once! People! Break their legs!

NERO

Bring the ladders!

FAUSTUS

Hit him so he dies!

CATILINE

He will never wake up again!

NERO

I want to send the other one out of this world. — He has his reward!

MARY

Oh! Jesus! You would not be so cruel to his body, will you?

MAGDALENE

Spare him! Spare him!

LONGINUS

Away! *(Longinus thrusts his lance into his side)*

MAGDALENE

Mary!

LONGINUS

Now take the bodies off the crosses!

QUINTUS

The body of the Galilean was given as a gift to this man, Joseph of Arimathea, by the governor.

CAIAPHAS

However, I will not allow him to be buried anywhere other than with the criminals.

LONGINUS

Since the body has been given to this man, it goes without saying that he can bury it however and wherever he wants.

ANNAS

So you still persist in your stubbornness, Joseph? You are not ashamed to honor the corpse of an executed criminal?

JOSEPH OF ARIMATHEA

I honor the person, the teacher sent to us by God, the innocently murdered. He did nothing wrong! And not a deceitful word left his mouth!

LONGINUS

People, our business is finished — we can go back!

Scene 4

JOHN

Finally, they are gone.

MAGDALENE

Take comfort, Mary! Look — now we are alone with our friends. The mockery and blasphemies have stopped.

MARY

Bring me my son! Look at him! Look at him! Mourn! Mourn! Cry for my child!

MAGDALENE

Mary! Remember the words he spoke when he left Bethany: „You will weep and wail. But the world will rejoice. You will be sad, but your sadness will be turned into joy, and your joy no one shall take from you!" Now he has finished his journey. His pain and suffering have come to an end. He went to his father.

SIMON OF BETHANY

O this man full of spirit and truth! How did he deserve such a fate?

MARY

Once in Bethlehem — now on Golgotha! My son, how your body is covered with blood and wounds! How the fury of your enemies has torn you apart! Lord, my God! You made his enemies triumph over him and increased the power of his opponents. Through his hands and feet they drove nails! His heart was pierced with a spear! Lord! Behold! Look at whom you have ruined! — I cry out, but my help is far away. My God, I call to you, but you do not answer. Our fathers hoped in you and were not forsaken. They cried out to you and were saved. Do not be far from me! May my strength hurry to my rescue! Save my soul!

JOHN

Look, Mother — peace rests on his face!

MARY

Peace also enters my heart. Look, son! The light came into the world. But you loved the darkness more than the light. God sent him to liberate the world through him. God loves the world so much that He gave His son! So that whoever believes in Him will never perish!

CHOIR

All of you,
who pass by,
stand still!
Watch and see:
Where can you find a love,
to equal this love?

XII. PRESENTATION
AT THE GRAVE

MAGDALENE

How happy I am to pay my last respects to the beloved Rabbi!

SALOME

Mary! But who will roll away the stone with which they closed the tomb?

MARY OF CLOPAS

The tomb is empty!

SALOME

Here still lie the cloths in which the body was wrapped — he no longer is in the grave!

ANGEL

What are you doing here so early in the morning?

MAGDALENE

We seek the one who was crucified to anoint him.

ANGEL

Why do you seek the living among the dead? He is not here, he has risen from the dead. He precedes you. You will see him as he told you.

MARY OF CLOPAS

Come, away from here!

SALOME

Let us rush to the city and tell them what has happened!

MARY OF CLOPAS

Mary, come with us!

MAGDALENE

No, leave me alone! Now the last comfort has been taken away from me.

ANGEL

Woman, why are you crying?

MAGDALENE

They have taken my master away and I do not know where they put him.

ANGEL

Woman, why are you crying? Who are you looking for?

MAGDALENE

If you took him away, tell me where you put him!

ANGEL

Mary! Go to your brothers and tell them: He has not yet ascended to his Father. But he will ascend to his Father and to your Father! To his God and to your God!

MAGDALENE

I know that my Savior lives!

ANGEL

Believe in the light so that you may become children of the light!

MAGDALENE

I will proclaim his resurrection to my brothers, in the midst of his congregation I will praise him! Wake up, Zion! Put on your best garments, Jerusalem, you holy city! People of Mount Zion, you who live in Jerusalem, wake up! Your eyes will behold the king in his beauty! Your ears will hear him!

He was condemned, shunned by people, a man in pain. But God freed him from the sorrows of death and raised him up. I know that my Savior lives!

He is with us everyday until the end of the world! That is why my heart rejoices, and my tongue exults! Oh, if only I could shout it through all the world, so that mountains and rocks and heaven and earth would echo with it:

Hallelujah! He is risen!

CHOIR

Hallelujah! The Lord, has overcome the powers of hell! He was not bound by death in the dark night of the grave! Sing to him in holy psalms! Scatter him the palms of victory!

Risen is the Lord!
Shout out praises to him, you heavens!
Sing to the victor, you O earth!
Hallelujah, to you, risen one!

Praise to you,who has overcome death,
you who died on Golgotha!
Praise to you, Savior of all sinners,
you who died on Golgotha!
Praise to you who at the altar of the cross
gave your life for us,
you have bought us for yourself,
only for you we live, only for you we die,

Hallelujah
Praise, glory, worship, power and splendor
to you from everlasting to everlasting!

Director	Christian Stückl
Stage and costume designer	Stefan Hageneier
Composer and Music Director	Markus Zwink
Deputy Director	Abdullah Kenan Karaca
Conductors	Eva Kammerer,
	Dr. Christian Wolf
Lighting Design	Günter E. Weiß

THE CAST

JESUS, THE APOSTLES AND HIS FAMILY

Jesus	Frederik Mayet
	Rochus Rückel
Peter	Benedikt Geisenhof
	Martin Güntner
Judas Iscariot	Cengiz Görür
	Martin Schuster
John	Anton Preisinger jr.
	Christoph Stöger
Thomas	Lukas Eberl
Andreas	Ferdinand Dörfler
James Zebedeus	Korbinian Freier
Simon the Zealot	Peter Mangold
Philip	Thomas Neu
Thaddaeus	Ruben Jondahl
Bartholomew	Nanno Hensold
James Alphaeus	Yannik Schaap
Matthew	Hubert Reiser
Mary, Mother of Jesus	Andrea Hecht
	Eva-Maria Reiser
Magdalene	Barbara Schuster
	Sophie Schuster
Simon of Bethany	Hubert Schmid
	Matthias Müller
Lazarus	Linus Wagner
Mary of Clopas	Viktoria Dörfler
Mary Salome	Lena Horak
Martha	Sarah Hesse
Simon, Brother of Jesus	Andreas Daisenberger
Joses, Brother of Jesus	Maximilian Bender
James, Brother of Jesus	Mario Backhausen

| *Angel* | David Bender |
| | Michael Hollatz |

HIGH COUNCIL

Caiphas	Andreas Richter
	Maximilian Karl Stöger
Annas	Walter Fischer
	Peter Stückl
Archelaus	Tobias Eich
	Simon Fischer
Nathanael	Kilian Clauß
	Sebastian Dörfler
Joseph of Arimathea	Christian Bierling
	Walter Rutz
Nicodemus	Abdullah Kenan Karaca
	Jonas Konsek
Ezekiel	Julius Iven
	Dima Schneider
Jehoshaphat	Florian Maderspacher
	Thomas Müller
Ammiel	Karl Führler
Ptolemy	Gregor Drohmann
Rabinth	Eugen Huber
Joshua	Franz Josef Freisl
Erez	Otto Huber
Aman	Gottfried Maderspacher
Gershon	Alexander Raggl
Ephraim	Korbinian Reiser
Ishmael	Christoph Maier

Erich Baab, Manfred Bauer, Karl Daisenberger, Dieter
Bruno Dashuber, Karl Eichhorn, Karl Geisenhof, Konrad
Gerold, Karl Härtle, Johann Mayr, Rudolf Neu, Georg
Rollnik, Theodor Schneller, Albert Schneller, Reinhart
Schorn, Arnulf Schuster, Bernd Sedlmaier, Johann Stückl,
Rudi Wolf, Rolf Zigon, Theo Zunterer, Anton Zwink

Dathan,	
Lord Chamerlain of Caiphas	Lucas Clauß
Esdras, servant of Caiphas	Kilian Wolf

SERVANTS OF CAIAPHAS

Lukas Delago, Leon Hagel, Lino Hensold, Quirin Maas, Felix Mangold, Lukas Schulte, Sebastian Schulte, Sebastian Ternes, Jakob Utschneider

PILATE, HIS WIFE AND SERVANTS

Pilate	Carsten Lück
	Anton Preisinger
Claudia, Pilate`s wife	Ursula Burkhart
Longinus, captain	Markus Köpf
	Ferdinand Meiler
Quintus	Soner Anılır
Pomponius	Wolfgang Proksch
Silvius	Maximilian Wagner
Flavius	Dionys Matthias Arnold
Claudius	Gunnar Eich

ROMAN SOLDIERS

Brutus	Johannes Müller
Pedius	Daniel Bartl
Milo	Stefan Königsberger
Domitius	Markus Rollnik
Gaius	Michael Güntner
Titus	Stefan Pongratz

Felix Arbogast, Andreas Brauchle, David Dedler, Daniel Markus Eich, Lukas Feichtner, Leonhard Fend, Tobias Fischer, Michael Fux, Kilian Gerold, Joseph Hofmann, Andreas Hugenschmidt, Thomas Huppmann, Martin Kessner, Leonhard Köpf, David Lampe, Johannes Maderspacher, Simon Mangold, Gregor Müller, Harald Niggl, Thomas Opfermann, Roman Papistock, Fabian Paulus, Nedim Pekhamarat, Andreas Pongratz, Johannes Michael Reiser, David Rutz, Sebastian Scheppan, Stefan Schmid, Simon Schötz, Stefan Schubert, Christoph Schweiger, Michael Seibold, Korbinian Stückl, Michael Tafaro, Thomas Utschneider, Dominikus Volk

Nero, executioner	Konrad Gerold
Catilina, executioner	Gürkan Özkan
Faustus, executioner	Valentin Rott
Agrippa, executioner	Patrick Voß

MERCHANTS

Albion	Benjamin Mayr
Booz	Mathias Feldmeier
Kosam	Christian Mayr
Ephod	Simon Marschall
Esrom	Josef Alois Feichtner

TEMPLEGUARDS

Selpha, captain	Michael Keßner
Panther	Christian Stoiber
Arphachshad	Julius Flemisch
Obed	Florian Swoboda
Balbus	Kilian Frühschütz
Malchus	Michael Drewing
Melchi	David Lück
Levi	Michael Stückl
Gidon	Jonathan Lück
Ram	Vito Backhausen
Kemuel	Stephan Bierling

Mallik Akinsola, Vinzenz Baab, Martin Dengg, Alexander
Deschler, Bibo Farman Haji, Bernhard Gimbel, Patrick
Haser, Alexander Hauptmann-Beyer, Ludwig Michael
Huber, Nikolaus Krach, Thomas Maderspacher, Leander
Marzell, Felix Müller, Andreas Riegg, Franz Rückel, Michele
Sandolo, Rohulla Taqizada, Aron Wilhelm, Ruslan Wjuchin

Hagar	Katrin Mangold
Sarah	Anja Swoboda
Judith	Monika Lück

KING HEROD AND HIS SERVANTS

Herod	Benedikt Fischer
	Simon Marschalek
Zabulon, Herod´s servant	Siegfried Biermeier
Manasses, Herod´s servant	Stephan Dörfler
Naasson, Herod´s servant	Nikolaus Krach
Delaja, Herod´s servant	Roland Kopic
Ehud, Herod´s servant	Korbinian Höldrich

Carina Bartl, Franziska Burger, Josephine Burkhart,
Christian Gerold, Franziska Anna Haertle, Martin Held,
Manuel Nitzsche, Tiziana Nötzli, Magdalena Rödl, Lena
Würsch

MEN AND WOMEN OF THE PEOPLE

Veronica	Ursula Mayr
Simon of Cyrene	Robert Heiland
Son of Simon of Cyrene	Kaldi Linz
Son of Simon of Cyrene	Jakob Maderspacher
Son of Simon of Cyrene	Kilian Wind
Gad, witness before the High Council	Arjuna Authenrieth
Eliab, witness before the High Council	Hamid Nikpai
Adulteress	Marina Kirchmayr
Barabbas	Mathias Feldmeier
Gestas	Benjamin Mayr
Dismas	Christian Mayr

Weeping Women
Veronika Baumann, Christine Fischer, Anna Maria
Gerold, Christine Gerum, Petra Lang, Lucia Müller,
Maria Papistock, Barbara Pongratz, Christine Renner-
Abdelhamed, Luisa Rott, Helga Stuckenberger, Monika
Stückl, Leni Müller, Sofie Müller

Passover Meal Servers	Vinzent Mayet
	Leonhard Schmid

PEOPLE AND CHILDREN OF JERUSALEM

CHORUS AND ORCHESTRA OF THE PASSIONPLAY 2022

Soprano

Soloists	Dominika Breidenbach,
	Maria Buchwieser,
	Katharina Osterhammer,
	Franziska Zwink,
	Maria Zwink

*Katharina Marie Bauer, Emma Burkhart, Lara Eisfeld, Simone
Eitzenberger, Antonie Eva Geisenhof, Anja Härtle, Magdalena
Hochenleitner, Janina Paloma Höldrich, Katharina Keller,
Theresa Koblitz, Annalena Köpf, Karina Köpf, Anna Norz,
Carla Ostler, Bernadette Ostler, Antonia Pfeffer, Nannette
Pongratz, Magdalena Ruppenthal, Caroline Schauer, Yvonne
Schmid, Barbara Schretter, Susanne Schwarz, Christine
Schwarz, Stephanie Seibold-Strobl, Leonie Seitz, Barbara*

Streibl, Martina Tschuri, Maria Franziska von Mücke, Annette
Wagner, Magdalena Wagner, Anja-Katharina Wolf, Marlene
Wolf

Alto

Soloists Caroline Fischer-Zwink, Monika Gallist, Veronika Pfaffenzeller, Antonie Schauer, Gabriele Weinfurter-Zwink

Angelika Angerer, Dorothea Barke, Lucia Bartl, Heike Bauer,
Margarete Beßenbacher, Paula Ehrmann, Zita Klara Anna
Feldmeier, Stefanie Fischer-Schauer, Ronja Fischer-Schauer,
Karolina Frank, Elisabeth Frank, Maria Fürsich, Maria Heiss,
Johanna Höldrich, Nina Höldrich, Franziska Huber, Carmen
Keller, Melanie Knöpfle, Anna-Lina Knufinke, Dorothea Lang,
Sabine Lehneis, Christine Marschalek, Irmgard Müller, Antonie
Müller, Eva Norz, Franziska Pongratz, Regina Raggl, Sarah
Reiter, Juliane Rollnik, Hannah Rutz, Elvira Schauer, Stephanie
Swoboda, Veronika Utschneider, Veronika Wagner, Diana Wolf

Tenor

Soloists Michael Etzel, Korbinian Heinzeller, Moritz Kugler, Michael Pfaffenzeller

Florian Alzinger, Angelo Brandelik, Paul Fellner,
Kilian Härtle, Franklin Hofmann, David Höldrich, Florian
Köpf, Josef Köpf, Luis Ernesto Mejia Lopez, Martin Mangold,
Lukas Ostler, Tobias Pfeiffer, Andreas Rödl, Julian Schwarz,
Florian Stückl, Marius Wagner, Albert Winkelbeiner, Vitus
Zwink

Bass

Soloists Heino Buchwieser, Anton Sonntag, Josef Zwink

Matthias Alexander Bauer, Elias Feldmeier, Tobias Fischer,
Bernhard Flemisch, Philipp Hauptmann, Raphael Höldrich,
Andreas Georg Kneifel, Vitus Norz, Martin Reiser, Robert Rott,
Peter Sachi, Valentin Schwarz, Joachim Späth, Jonas Stanek,
David Stanek, Simeon Stanek, Quirin Streibl, Markus Stückl,
Ludwig Utschneider, Hermann Wind, Simon Wind, Laurenz
Zwink

Concertmaster	Angelika Lichtenstern
	Barbara Schenk
	Therese Storck

Violoncello Soloists	Gregor Babica,
	Laura Buchwieser,
	Andreas Fischer

1. Violin

Daniela Achilles-Widenhorn, Christina Bomblies, Julia
Burkart, Luca Carli, Tercia Oliveira da Silva, Pedro
Fioramonte, Thomas Floßmann, Elisabeth Gossner,
Patricia Hibler, Karl Kemper, Daniela Kemper, Beate
Kirchbichler, Johannes sen. Klucker, Elisabeth Lang,
Stefanie Pfaffenzeller, Michael sen. Pfaffenzeller, Johanna
Raeder, Julika Storck, Maria Gruber, Renate Walter

2. Violin

Antonia Budion, Martin Deubel, Ingeborg Eblenkamp,
Dominika Gansler, Angela Gilgenreiner, Elisabeth
Gossner, Margit Huber, Sophia Kees, Beate Kirchbichler,
Elisabeth Klucker, Inga Kröger, Alexandra Lenzen,
Theresa Meichsner, Sandra Paulus, Sophie Pfaffenzeller,
Peter Renner, Anita Stanek, Irmgard Tralmer, Luise
Tschuri, Annalena Wank, Nina Wörndle, Laura Zwink

3. Violin

Johanna Fellner, Viktoria Fuksova, Andreas Magold,
Katharina Müller, Magdalena Müller, Julia Sedlmaier

Viola

Eve Abraham, Barbara Emslander-Gayler, Sandor Farkas,
Katharina Floßmann, Oksana Gessner, Pia Janner-
Horn, Klaus-Dieter Kunzmann, Martina Maderspacher,
Katharina Schellhorn, Bodil Schnurrer, Hedwig Simet,
Veronika Steinel, Amelie Stoiber

Violoncello
Gregor Babica, Laura Elizabeta Crnojevic, Charlotte Henkel, Bruno Hilz, Benedikt Huber, Veronika Kammermeier, Edgar Schumann, Jonathan Stroh, Heinrich Zehentbauer

Double Bass
Markus Baumann, Uwe Einzmann, Max sen. Floßmann, Maximilian jun. Floßmann, Josef Gilgenreiner, Jennifer Hoffmann, Magdalena Hosp, Anton Kammermeier, Teresa Weiler

Flute
Emily Pfeiffer, Marianne Saal, Simone Steiner, Bianca Wind

Oboe
Birgit Bauer, Lisa Best, Michaela Bocklet, Olivija Popovaite, Georg Schweinberger, Magdalena Steinbauer, Jeannine Wimmer, Anselm Wohlfahrt

Clarinet
Florian Härtle, Natalie Huppmann, Alexandra Lim, Florian Mangold, Arno Maczioch, Carmen Rodriguez-Hitschfeld, Franziska Schweiger

Bassoon
Matthias Delazer, Leo Kohler, Bettina Peschanel, Marco Scidá, Raphael Sirch, Christoph Wandinger

Horn
Jonathan Baur, Stefan Buchwieser, Tobias Haseidl, Mario Löhde, Christoph Lutz, Gerhard Schöber

Trumpet
Dagmar Conrady, Barbara Daisenberger, Josef Lechner, Ernst Maderspacher, Florian Nowak, Josef jun. Pongratz, Vinzenz Pongratz

Trombone
Kai Begemann, Johannes Hornsteiner, Bernhard Hufnagl, Manfred Klieber, Luis Neuner, Valentin Stoiber, Andreas von Mücke

Kettledrum
Matthias Baumann, Severin Schauer, Tobias Schauer

Technical Direction	Carsten Lück, Martin Feichtner
Production Assistant	Kilian Clauß
Stage and costume assistant	Elena Scheicher, Lorenz Stöger
Chorus- und Orchestra office	Michael Pfaffenzeller, Franziska Zwink

Tailoring and costume editing

Management, Model and section development	Susanne Eski
Production Manager	Anna Schories
Pattern Cutter	Anneliese Adelwart-Schedler, Christiane Gassler, Ines Kern, Sabine Marzell

Tailoring
Karin Anders, Maria Beßenbacher, Annelies Buchwieser, Angelika Deschler, Lisa Flori, Monika Günther, Sylvia Heinzeller, Magdalena Hosp, Kirstin Luhmer, Rosemarie Pongratz, Irma Rauch, Luisa Rott, Sara Sadoun, Manuela Schultes, Cäcilia Schwander, Maria-Magdalena Soukup, Tristan Szcesny, Ursula Wagner, Christl Wallinger, Edith Wörz, Adelinde Zencominierski

Costume editing and dyeing	Jimena Oviedo, Jonna Carstensen, Lisa Lauren, Waltraud Münzhuber, Malena Modeer, Helena Segl

Head of Wardrobe	Rosemarie Pongratz
Shoemaker	Firma Harr, Firma Hiegl
Costumes for romans and executioner	Klaus Frech
Modiste	Alida Buchböck, Andrea Fippl, Emilie Prosty
Saddler	Felix Niggl
Armours, Jewellery	Waltraud Münzhuber, Felix Niggl
Make-up artist	Lena Bader, Katrin Zindl

Stage construction/ Carpentry

Workshop management   Florian Bartl
Supervisor   Simon Bartl

Michael Adam, Lorenz Bierling, Toni Dittrich, Ferdinand Dörfler, Tobias Eich, Roman Feldmeier, Peter Hensold, Thomas Höck, Benjamin Mayr, Alan Reid, Valentin Rott, Johanna Zehentbauer

Scene painting   Atelier Schmidbauer,
Christian Huber,
Martin von Mücke,
Alejandro Valbuena,
Pascuale Mele

Lighting
Head of Lighting   Martin Feichtner
Simon Bartl,
Mathias Feldmeier,
Thilo Feldmeier,
Christian Marzell
Hannes Gambeck,
Rainer Ludwig,
Godowin Zunke

Sound

Fa. Neumann& Müller (Rudolf Pirc), Müller BBM
(Gunther Engel), Marc Heene, Maximilian Kasseckert,
Christoph Müller, Ekki von Nordenskjöld, Toni Sprikl

Props

Leader Sarah Hesse
Carina Bartl, Viktoria Bischl, Barbara Daisenberger,
Katharina von Aigner, Michaela Gräper, Stefanie
Hallerbach, Toni Henningfeld, Veronika Karlstetter,
Anne Mack

Sculptor

Leader Tobias Haseidl
Quirin Beyerle, Christian Bierling, Armin Hecht, Veronika
Hecht, Jonas Heidle, Ludwig Huber, Magdalena Rödl,
Jonas Strobl

Weapons Metal construction	Martin Breidenbach, Peter Glass, Anton Wiedemann

Stage

Leader Peter Maderspacher
Side stage master Anton Hochenleitner, Christoph Zwink

Stage construction

Aaron Albl, Michael Albl, Lorenz Bierling, Christoph
Blaschke, Simon Filser, Franz Handschuh, Martin
Harbauer, Michael Hässler, Fabian Hawxby, Kevin Heinle,
Robin Heinle, Peter Hensold, Daniela Höldrich, Rudi
Höldrich, Herbert Köpf, Pirmin Kröker, Benjamin Lampe,
Manuel Leendertz, Hannelore Maderspacher, Carlo
Margraf, Elias Marzell, Florian Misniks, Sebastian Mützel,
Wilson Quinchimbla, Wolfgang Reicherl, Jacob Reid,
Robert Reindl, Johannes Reiser, Florian Richter, Gregor
Schneller, Tobias Schneller, Georg Schwarz, Florian Stückl,
Markus Stückl, Egbert von der Höh, Sebastian Wagner,
Robin Wankmüller, Mario Wolff, Martin Zigon

Doorman Hermann Wiegand

Voice training for performers	Andreas Sippel
Voice training for singers	Johannes Gruber
	Gabriele Weinfurter-Zwink
Editing of vocal texts	Gabriele Weinfurter-Zwink
Note grafic	Benedikt Huber

PRESS AND PUBLIC RELATIONS

Leader	Frederik Mayet
	Jenny Greza,
	Franziska Seher
Staff members	Maximilian Mayet,
	Karen Pfann

House manager and guest relations	Birgit Reiser,
	Carla Speer
Managing Director of the Passion Play	Walter Rutz
Deputy Managing Director	Monika Stückl

PLAYING DAYS

Premiere: Saturday May 14, 2022

Spieltage: Tuesday, Thursday, Friday, Saturday, Sunday

May 14 - August 14   1st part 14.30 p.m.– 5.00 p.m.
                            2nd part 8.00 p.m. – 10.30 p.m.

Break approx. between 5.00 p.m. and 8.00 p.m.
End of the performance approx. 10.30 p.m.

August 15 - October 2   1st part 1.30 p.m. – 4.00 p.m.
                            2nd part 7.00 p.m. - 9:30 h

Break approx. between 4.00 p.m. and 7.00 p.m.
End of the performance approx. 9.30 p.m.

May	June	July	August	September	October
	Th 02.			Th 01.	
	Fr 03.	Fr 01.		Fr 02.	
	Sa 04.	Sa 02.		Sa 03.	Sa 01.
	Su 05.	Su 03.		Su 04.	Su 02.
	Mo 06.				
	Tu 07.	Tu 05.	Tu 02.	Tu 06.	
	Th 09.	Th 07.	Th 04.	Th 08.	
	Fr 10.	Fr 08.	Fr 05.	Fr 09.	
	Sa 11.	Sa 09.	Sa 06.	Sa 10.	
	Su 12.	Su 10.	Su 07.	Su 11.	
	Tu 14.	Tu 12.	Tu 09.	Tu 13.	
	Th 16.	Th 14.	Th 11.	Th 15.	
	Fr 17.	Fr 15.	Fr 12.	Fr 16.	
Sa 14.	Sa 18.	Sa 16.	Sa 13.	Sa 17.	
Su 15.	Su 19.	Su 17.	Su 14.	Su 18.	
Tu 17.	Tu 21.	Tu 19.	Tu 16.	Tu 20.	
Th 19.	Th 23.	Th 21.	Th 18.	Th 22.	
Fr 20.	Fr 24.	Fr 22.	Fr 19.	Fr 23.	
Sa 21.	Sa 25.	Sa 23.	Sa 20.	Sa 24.	
Su 22.	Su 26.	Su 24.	Su 21.	Su 25.	
Tu 24.	Tu 28.	Tu 26.	Tu 23.	Tu 27.	
Th 26.	Th 30.	Th 28.	Th 25.	Th 29.	
Fr 27.		Fr 29.	Fr 26.	Fr 30.	
Sa 28.		Sa 30.	Sa 27.		
Su 29.		Su 31.	Su 28.		
Tu 31.			Tu 30.		

Stay
in contact

PASSION
PLAY
OBERAMMERGAU

passionplayoberammergau

Passionsspiele_oberammergau

PassionsspieleOberammergau

Subscribe to the newsletter

2022
PASSIONS
SPIELE
OBERAMMERGAU

OFFICIAL
MERCHANDISE

shop.passionsspiele-oberammergau.de

2017
DER FLIEGENDE HOLLÄNDER
Oper von Richard Wagner

2013
MOSES
von Feridun Zaimoglu
und Günter Senkel

2011
JOSEPH UND SEINE BRÜDER
nach Thomas Mann

Auch im Sommer 2023 erwartet Sie im assionstheater Oberammergau eine neue Inszenierung.

www.passionstheater.de

2014
EIN SOMMERNACHTSTRAUM
von William Shakespeare

Nature Park Ammergau Alps

Since 2017 the Ammergauer Alps are proud to be a certified Nature Park. Five different habitats on 227 km² give a home to rare species and animals worthy to be protected.
The torrential river Ammer, the Rochusfeld marshlands or the lonesome mixed mountain forest in the Graswang Valley are just three examples for the unique environment around the six Nature Park towns Bad Bayersoien, Bad Kohlgrub, Saulgrub, Unterammergau, Oberammergau and Ettal.

www.ammergau-alps.com

Order souvernirs of the Oberammergau Passion Play or the Ammergau Alps Nature Park online:

Nature Park
Ammergau Alps

d carving

Culture & Tradition

Among the Oberammergau
Passion Play, the castle of King
Ludwig II, Linderhof Palace
with its gorgeous gardens and
the Benedictine Abbey in Ettal
are the cultural highlights of
the Nature Park Region.
Ettal Monastery is famous for
its impressing basilica and the
monasterial brewery, produc-
ing since 1609.

rhof Palace

Ettal Monastery

Traditional Folk Dancer

Frescos in Oberammergau

e sure to visit the historic
aintings on the house walls
hile in the region! These
ncient frescos are called
üftlmalerei".
terested in arts and crafts?
ating back to the middle
ges, but still today the wood
arving tradition is alive.

View from the Laber mountain

Easy summiting

Simply take one of the chairlifts or cable cars - that's just a facile way to enjoy the fantastic panoramic view into the mountains or to the Zug- spitze - Germanys' highe peak.

Walking the trails

Of course, the peaks of the two-thousanders might be luring for am- bitious hikers. But a walk on the Altherrenweg trail with a local snack stop is just as promising as it is enjoyable.

Along the Ammergau Alps Meditation Trail

On tour in the Graswang Valley

...or riding by bike

Approximately 500km lc is the network for cyclin The roads and paths link cultural spots with the beautiful landscape of tl Ammergau Alps.
Local renting stations of MTBs, touring and e-bik

Hiking above the clouds

Nature Park
Ammergau Alps

Enjoyment and relaxation

Its not only the fresh air and the unspoilt views. Also comfort offers such as yoga classes, massages and a combination of balanced nutrition and culinary delights create a real holiday feeling.

Health experts provide personal advices, for example healing peat baths with the regional mud against joint pain and dorsalgia.

(IM) MATERIA L

F A B R I C
B O D Y and
P A S S I O N

1634

The cloth cube will be dismantled in the middle of October and the individual panels, which can be reserved and purchased from the 30th April onwards, are handed over to the buyers.

(IM)MATERIAL –
fabric, body and passion

An installation marking the 2022 Passion Play

23 April – 16 October 2022

The Oberammergau Museum, one of the most important cultural history museums in Bavaria, is being transformed into a spectacular complete work of art with building and space installations as well as an exhibition for the 42nd Passion Play with the title „(IM)MATERIAL – Fabric, Body and Passion".

A large blue cube, made of the costumes worn by the lay actors of the Passion Play 2000 and 2010, cloaks the building and slices through the rooms within. The new tapestry-like walls transform the 1910 museum into an art object clearly visible from afar. The fabric stretches in the interior across all three floors, creating new spatial structures: a normal *outside* and an *inside*, which is distorted and unfamiliar. The visitor wanders between these worlds, entering and leaving the cube. Within, a small selection of exhibits are highlighted, exhibition objects are wrapped, changed and subjected to light projections. The core of the collection are wooden sculptures over four centuries that take as their theme the life, suffering, the fears, worries and the hopes of people and relate them to the Passion. By focussing the collection, the museum becomes a place of reflection on regional, cultural and societal notions and character. The route through the exhibition begins at the crib section and leads through the historic rooms on the first floor, ending with a projection and sound installation in the roof space. On leaving, the visitor is given a piece of the cloth taken from the 2000 and 2010 Passion costumes – a symbol for (im)material exchange and community amongst people.

Opening times
April 23 – May 13 Tuesday – Sunday 10 am – 5 pm

May 14 – August 14
On performance days: 9 am – 2 pm and 5 pm – 7:30 pm
On non-performance days (Monday, Wednesday): 9 am – 6 pm

August 15 – October 2
On performance days: 9 am – 1 pm and 4 pm – 6:30 pm
On non-performance days (Monday, Wednesday): 9 am – 6 pm

October 3 – October 16 Tuesday – Sunday 10 am – 5 pm

Oberammergau Museum | Dorfstraße 8 | 82487 Oberammergau
www.oberammergaumuseum.de

Mut hat viele Seiten.

Mut ist aufmerksam.

Mut bringt Licht ins Dunkel.

Mut ist unbequem.

Mut schaut hin.

Mut hört zu.

Mut fragt nach.

Mut entscheidet.

Mut deckt auf.

Mut bewegt.

Mut verändert.

Mut ist unabhängig.

Mut macht neugierig.

Mut ist solidarisch.

Mut sieht mehr.

Süddeutsche Zeitung

Mut verbindet.

Wer die Welt liebt, **hört ihr zu.**

Jeden Morgen faszinierende Einblicke für Neugierige.

Jetzt reinhören: ab 6.05 Uhr **im Radio** oder jederzeit **auf bayern2.de**

BR | BAYERN 2